LIVING
LEARNING

Lessons of Insight and Encouragement on the Path of Motherhood

Gail Cawley Showalter

Requests for such permission should be addressed to:
Gail Cawley Showalter 152 Grand Chase Nederland, TX 77627 USA

Cover designed by Murshidi Mahmud

Manufactured in the United States of America

979-8-9876834-1-5 (Kindle)
979-8-9876834-2-2 (EPUB)
979-8-9876834-0-8 (Paperback)

Publisher's Cataloging-in-Publication data
Names: Showalter, Gail Cawley, author.
Title: Living learning loving / Gail Cawley Showalter.
Description: Nederland, TX: Gail Showalter, 2023.

Identifiers: LCCN: 2023901376 | ISBN: 979-8-9876834-0-8 (paperback) | 979-8-9876834-1-5 (Kindle) | 979-8-9876834-2-2 (epub) Subjects: LCSH Parenting. | Self help. | BISAC SELF-HELP / Personal Growth / Happiness | SELF-HELP / Spiritual | FAMILY & RELATIONSHIPS / Parenting / Motherhood Classification: LCC HQ759 .S56 2023 | DDC 306.874/3--dc23

In Praise of Living Learning Loving

What Readers are Saying:

Living Learning Loving is the perfect title for Gail Showalter's book on single parenting. Readers will find a solid resource in this lively and encouraging text, which will equip women in their new role of single mom. Showalter offers real-life stories, real-life lessons, and real-life successes so that moms everywhere can learn to live as joyful overcomers just as God has intended.

—Michele Howe
Author of Burden Lifters and Faith, Friends
and Other Flotation Devices Reviewer/Columnist
https://www.michelehowe.wordpress.com

Gail Cawley Showalter weaves honesty and wisdom throughout *Living Learning Loving: Lessons of Insight and Encouragement on the Path of Motherhood*. Both veteran single mothers and those recently thrust into this unfamiliar role will appreciate her personal stories and practical steps for transitioning into this new life. Journaling questions in each chapter are perfect for personal growth or group discussion.

—Sandra P. Aldrich
Author of Heart Hugs for Single Moms: 52 Devotions
to Encourage You Colorado Springs, Colorado
http://www.sandraaldrich.com

Gail Showalter has a wealth of knowledge and a strong understanding of the challenges of single moms because she has lived it. She uses personal stories, her struggles and what she learned through those years to skillfully give single moms hope in their journey. Her desire to encourage and equip those looking for answers is evident in her book, *Living Learning Loving.*

—Robyn Besemann
Author, Singer/Songwriter, Inspirational Speaker, Radio Show Host
https://twitter.com/robynbmin?lang=en

No matter where you are in your single-mother life, in this book you'll find the encouragement needed for the journey. Gail Showalter is an excellent storyteller, gifted with words of wisdom and humor. You'll love the guided questions at the end of each chapter, a perfect small group study.

—Pam Kanaly
Speaker, Author of The Single Mom and Her Rollercoaster Emotions, and National Mother of Achievement Honoree
https://www.amazon.com/stores/Pam-Kanaly/author/B00JEB1RAS

You will immediately feel a connection to Gail as she shares her heart for single moms and anyone else who is facing great challenges. She speaks from personal experience, a deep and abiding faith, and an optimism forged through difficult circumstances. Gail's writing will bring strength, endurance, and hope for your journey!

—Rev. James R. Fuller, Ph.D.
Former Senior Pastor, Calder Baptist Church, Beaumont, Texas

Gail has been passionate about single moms and the challenges they face for many, many years. Having been a single parent herself, she is quite familiar with the unique struggles and joys of raising children without the consistent help of a spouse. Gail's ministry has been continuous and effective throughout the years, and she has become one of the leading thinkers and voices for ministry to single moms in the U. S.

—Dennis Franck

Author, Coach, Consultant, Musician, and Speaker: Equipping Leaders, Young Adults, Single Adults & Their Families

https://www.facebook.com/franckinsights

Dedicated

To Treva, Damon, and Lance, my three children
who have taught and continue to
teach me so much.

Acknowledgments

This book would never have been written
without the undying support of my husband, Sam.
He accepts me, as I am, warts and all.
He encourages me to express myself and gives me a voice.

Contents

Always
Live
Learn
&
Love !

Gail

Introduction

The 2021 U. S. census revealed out of 11 million custodial parents in the United States, nearly 80% are single mothers who are attempting to be the best moms they can be for their children.[1]

There are many reasons why there are more single-parent homes than ever before: divorce or leaving an abusive relationship, choosing not to marry, death of a spouse, or opting to be a single parent from the start. For some people, it isn't even their choice, but the fact is, many parents are single-handedly raising children alone, and that is why this book was written.

As a woman who has been through a divorce and who parented three children for sixteen years, I have learned a few survival skills in the process and believe life is all about growth and letting experience be one of the best teachers that life can offer. I know firsthand how important it is to have a bit of guidance from someone who has been there, done that.

The lessons in this book are from my personal journey—stories that get straight to the point, offering inspiration, motivation, and practical solutions to single parenting issues.

Even if you aren't technically "single" but find yourself shouldering most of the child-rearing load, this book will touch on topics that you also face each day as the primary caregiver. You will discover new ways to view your challenges, handle difficult situations, and make changes that work in your favor.

Each chapter has tips and SMORE (Single Mothers: Overjoyed, Rejuvenated, & Empowered) to consider for further contemplation. This book is designed to be used as a personal journal or group study guide. I pray for success for your journey.

Gail—"An old bird with a soft spot for single moms."

Gail's passion for single moms motivated her to establish SMORE for Women, a nonprofit whose goal is:

Single Moms: Overjoyed, Rejuvenated, & Empowered!

Gail's personal journey has brought her over many rough roads: having three children in three years, a divorce when they were three, four, and five-years-old, a serious illness of a child, going back to college with three young children in tow, and personal chronic illness. She knows the struggles, heartaches, and the day-to-day challenges of being "head of a household."

To contact Gail:
Email: gail@gailshowalter.com
Phone: 409-718-0285
Website: https://www.gailshowalter.com/

CHAPTER ONE

Living with Solitude

Instead of viewing aloneness as a shameful condition to cure, think of it as one of freedom and opportunity.

THE STORY YOU TELL YOURSELF

—Lauren Mackler, *Soulmate*

I had relapsed with the flu and was completely drained. Then I opened the envelope. "Divorce" screamed out at me. Here I was in our king-sized bed with my three children playing somewhere in our large dream home. But this was not a dream. I cried out my last tears. Then I threw up. Alone—again.

Not all divorce is the disaster I thought mine was. I had friends who needed to get divorced. I couldn't see it for me, however. Our marriage had been a good one until, well, until it wasn't.

Ironically, I was familiar with solitude. Mothering three children born in a three-year period, I was seldom alone. Solitude is different. It's in the mind.

Being alone gets a bad rap. Often, being alone has a negative connotation, as if something is wrong with you if you are alone. You enter a restaurant, for example, and the hostess says, "Just one?" as if there is something wrong with being just one. Our world is geared for pairs.

Even though being single should not carry any undertone at all, our culture continues to support the notion that a single woman must have a flaw or be gay. Not so for the single man. That is the myth. Single mothers are not flawed. They are competent, hard-working, loving women who carry a heavy load.

Another myth that plagues too many single women is their search for a man to "complete" them. As in *The Missing Piece Meets the Big O* by Shel Silverstein[2], single women must learn to "roll" alone before searching

COMPLEMENT

to be completed by another. As a single mom, you may be lonely if only occasionally. You may not be living the life you had planned. One single mom told me, "I have been a single mom for ten years now. My daughter is in sixth grade, things are going well, but I'm thirty-five years old and aching to find a suitable partner and maybe have another child. I envy those who have their complete and blossoming family while I am alone raising my child." Surely many women raising children alone could say this.

Most women don't plan to be a single parent. For many, difficulties and disappointments are frequent events during the parenting process. As with most rough journeys in life, there is much to be learned on these trips. There are, however, some gems that can be polished only when you are alone. It may mean traveling some treacherous roads. You may have to make some heart-wrenching decisions. I've spent many days in solitude—some by choice, others not. Either way, I learned more, stretched more, and grew more during those times. Aloneness need not be lonely. It can be a time for needed change and insight into your life. Many of our great spiritual leaders were imprisoned and wrote inspired words while in solitude.

I used to wonder why people wanted to climb mountains, especially considering all the dangers involved. Now I can see it as overcoming a great challenge or obstacle. Isn't that what you do daily? Aren't you overcoming challenges and obstacles and sometimes wondering what your next step will be? Or worrying if you will make it through the next crisis? Being alone can be an opportunity to reach out and learn from new experiences. A single woman and dear friend told me of one of her experiences.

"I own a circular saw, and I use it too. I put my safety glasses on, really think about where and how I'm cutting my board, and I go for it. And . . . I'm the proud creator of a set of closet shoe shelves that look good and are so wonderfully efficient . . . if I do say so myself. That may not seem like a big deal to some. I mean, HGTV testifies to the fact that women can be carpenters too. But for me, it was a big deal. I grew up with the understanding that circular saws, drills, and nail guns were Daddy's tools and that basically a circular saw was too dangerous for me to handle. Since I was single and without the manly power of a husband, and I had limited resources of help, I could feel rather alone in my situation. I'm also hesitant to ask others for help, so I would lament over the fact that I just wanted some boards cut. Buying and learning to use a circular saw was only one of many things that would challenge me in my singleness. There have been other things in my life that I have tackled alone, even as I confronted my feelings of discomfort or inadequacy—house decisions, auto repairs, and speaking in front of a large group." Becoming your own person requires taking time away from the crowd and answering the hard questions. It's a process that demands time apart. Once you are sure of yourself, your beliefs, and your convictions, the decisions you make will be wiser and more appropriate for your life. Maybe we don't want to look within. Maybe it is painful for us to think about our loss or hurt. Maybe we just don't enjoy being by our self. Taking it a small bite at a time is easier than going away alone for a long weekend. Try going to the mall, going for a walk, or eating in the park alone. Use the time deliberately. Consider taking a notepad with you to write down thoughts that come to you. You may be surprised what you learn. And you may get a much-needed break from the chaos of your life.

Allow your soul to be fertile ground for the seeds of spiritual growth. Growth is what life is about. If you haven't noticed, look at your children. Aren't you always buying new shoes and jeans? Seasons change, and growth continues. Spiritual growth does not happen automatically. As adults, we should ask ourselves how we have grown spiritually of late. Are you the same person you were a year ago? What have you learned? How would others say you are different?

The Amazing Grace of Aloneness

When I was born, my siblings were eight, twelve, and sixteen. Much too old to want to play with me. I spent my early years entertaining myself. I spent many hours in solitude. Later in life after a divorce, with three young children, I craved time alone. And then I resented it passionately when it came. It was like the anticipation of a delicious meal with its aroma and enticement and then the unpleasant indigestion that follows after over indulging my appetite.

Never confuse this: being alone is not the same as being lonely. Perhaps the fear of loneliness keeps you from experiencing the grace of aloneness. As a single mom, you may feel lonely, especially if you are often alone. Perhaps this is not the life you had dreamed of. Difficulties and disappointments faced alone can be daily events for single mothers. There are, however, some gems that can be polished when we are alone.

Being alone brings a grace all its own. Grace is often explained as "unmerited favor." In other words, something good that happens to us that we don't deserve. There is grace that comes to you when you are alone that cannot come any other way. The following are points of grace you can experience when you are willing to accept aloneness as a pathway to inner peace.

G—Growth is what spiritual life is about. You may avoid it because growth is painful. For the seed to sprout, it must first crack open.

If you haven't noticed, look around. Physical growth is a constant. Spiritual growth, not so much. We should ask ourselves how we have grown lately. Am I the same person I was a year ago? What have I learned? Would others say I was different?

R—Refresh. Aloneness can renew, refresh, and give us valuable reflection. Living an alone life requires more work for those who experience it. There is stress, sometimes overwhelming stress, especially for those who are single adults raising children. Our great spiritual teachers all spent time away from crowds. So should we. Take the time to refresh. Reflect on your goals for your life.

A—Acceptance is powerful. Mary, the mother of Jesus, wondered, "How can this be?" And then quickly accepted, "Let it be." Truly accepting God's will is the essence of prayer. Yet for us, it seems an insurmountable feat.

Once my daughter accepted that she was not able to conceive, she was open to adoption. Our lovely granddaughter is grown now, and we can't imagine our lives without our beautiful "baby" from Russia. When you arrive at the place where you are no longer attempting to fix, control, blame, judge, or persuade others, you have reached acceptance.

C—Compassion is usually developed after we experience a valley of our own. It wasn't until after my father's death that I realized it was important to be there for my friends when they lose a loved one. After the heartache of divorce, my compassion for single mothers developed into a passion. We are creatures designed to have empathy for others.

E—Education is a terrific journey to take when alone. Learning something new can change your entire perspective. Learning comes in many forms. A new hobby requires learning. Career development demands acquiring new knowledge. It is so much easier to read a book when you are alone.

One of my greatest adventures was returning to college with three small children in tow. My very first published article was about that experience.

Aloneness is not all bad. It can be a time for great insight and changes in your life. Being alone can be an opportunity to try new experiences. Bruce Wilkinson, the author of *The Dream Giver*, says, "Unfortunately, many people have never come to this, because they've never ventured beyond where they feel safe. These people will seldom, if ever, see God working powerfully in their lives."[3]

Don't you want to see God working powerfully in your life? Take the time to be alone. Allow aloneness to perch on a branch in your soul so you can experience its amazing grace.

You can enjoy solitude without being lonely.

The difference between solitude and loneliness is deep and wide. Solitude is a treasure that opens a world to our souls. You can enjoy solitude without being lonely. Solitude restores and can even be liberating. It can be an opportunity to transform your life, a time to listen to the Spirit within.

Solitude suggests peacefulness stemming from a state of inner richness. It is a means of enjoying the quiet and whatever it brings that is satisfying and from which we draw sustenance. It is something we cultivate. Solitude is refreshing, an opportunity to renew ourselves. In other words, it replenishes us.[4]

—Hara Estroff Marano

Once you learn to embrace solitude, your spiritual life will grow by leaps and bounds. It is the perfect time to hear the still small voice speak to your situation.

If we want to hear the Friend within, we must be quiet and still, embrace the solitude, meditate, and drink it in.

When God gets us alone by affliction, heartbreak or temptation, by disappointment, sickness, or by thwarted affection, by broken friendship, or by a new friendship-when He gets us absolutely alone, and we are dumbfounded, and cannot ask one question, then He begins to expound (speak).[5]

—Oswald Chambers

How do you handle being alone? How do you embrace solitude? Can you accept time alone as an opportunity for growth?

(See Appendix I for a spiritual exercise.)

SMORE TO CONSIDER

How do you feel about being alone?
[ ] Love it
[ ] Hate it   70% / 30%.
[ ] Not sure   content.

Describe a time when being alone was peaceful.

In what ways do you embrace solitude?
[✓] Reading
[✓] Journaling
[ ] Surrounded by nature
[ ] Taking a long soak in the tub or shower

Describe a new activity you are willing to try in which you can experience a solitude that refreshes your soul.

London trips, learn, live, tranquility alone in room.

Name two areas where you would like to see "profound growth."

Better boundaries
More self love n care.

Describe what that growth would look like.
(If you can see it—you can do it.)

CHAPTER TWO

Living with Boundaries

Your personal boundaries protect the inner core of your identity and your right to choices.

—Gerard Manley Hopkins, *Boundaries*

Of all the boundaries that surround us, our internal ones are the most confusing, complex, and conflicting. When you fail to control your personal habits, issues, and maybe even addictions, you open yourself up to experiencing shame and embarrassment. This could be something as simple as keeping your opinions to yourself or as complex as abstaining from a controlled substance. While it seems easy to tell others how to solve their problems, we have a tough time with our own internal and often private tormentors.

When we experience shame, embarrassment, along with a host of other bad feelings, we implement coping strategies: out-of-control eating or not eating, inability to manage our time or money, and at times, even inappropriate sexual behaviors.

When we use these poor coping strategies, it compounds all our bad feelings, and we may be tempted to isolate ourselves and continue the behaviors in private, quiet places where no one can see us, or so we think. The more we isolate ourselves, the harder our struggle becomes, because just as an untreated cancer can become life threatening in a short time, poor coping strategies will worsen with time, increasing the feelings of shame, hopelessness, and isolation.

Brené Brown says in her book *The Gifts of Imperfection*, "Shame is the intensely painful feeling or experience of believing we are flawed and therefore unworthy of love and belonging."[6]

If you are experiencing shame, you may have pulled away from many of your relationships, but the fact of the matter is, we need relationships in order to survive.

In the book *Boundaries*, Dr. Henry Cloud and Dr. John Townsend identify three reasons we have trouble controlling our own problems:

- We try to use willpower to solve boundary problems.
- We are our own worst enemies.
- We withdraw from relationships.[7]

In order to embrace our personal strengths, emotional needs, and yes, even our struggles, we need to understand how boundaries can help create safety zones in our lives.

We may be under the impression that it all depends on our own determination, that it's simply a matter of willpower. This approach can make an idol out of the will, which is something God never intended. We could learn a lesson from the Easter story where Jesus says, "Not my will, but yours be done" (Luke 22:42, New International Version). We think we know what's best for us and others just don't understand our situation.

When I think back to my first marriage, I must have been compensating for something that wasn't working right or not meeting my personal needs, because I can see where I took absolute control over several areas in my life. The need to control something in my life led me to implement the SHE (Sidetracked Home Executives) program, which was a highly ordered system of household maintenance and cleaning that you can still find online. I found this to be an attractive challenge that appealed to my personality's natural willpower and persistence. I threw myself wholeheartedly into it.

Sometimes other people's inability to meet our needs, emotional or physical, leads to disappointments—sometimes painfully deep disappointments—so it becomes easier to just rely on our own abilities to ward off the pain.

You might think that being independent means you have protected yourself against being hurt or disappointed because of someone else's failures, but that's not true. Dogged independence often means you are afraid to acknowledge you may have limitations or weaknesses. Most fiercely independent people wouldn't consider themselves fearful, but it is fear, bolstered by pride, that keeps them from asking others for help. This behavior becomes a barricade instead of a boundary in relationships. Not knowing how to establish sensible boundaries can have an adverse effect on relationships; instead of bringing a couple closer, it can build huge walls that are hard to get over.

I needed healthy boundaries and a clearer understanding that I had family members and friends who would help, to say nothing of the fact that I had a divine creator who loved me and was willing to "work [things] together for [my] good" (Rom. 8:28, King James Version). I just needed to let loose of the controls.

Many seminar leaders and motivational speakers stress the power of self-will as the solution to whatever causes your problems. They tell us to depend on our willpower to eat sensibly, to manage money wisely, to balance time with families, and to cope with all the other boundary problems we face. If this were the answer to our personal issues, then we who like to control our world would have figured it out by now.

We don't always know how out of balance our boundaries are until they are challenged. Rebuilding a marriage or going through a divorce are some of the times that expose where our boundary lines lay and where they need to change.

During my divorce, the negotiations seemed to go on forever. My first husband, Robert, was livid about the fact that I wasn't pushing things along from my end. Frankly, I didn't want a divorce and didn't care how long it took him to get one. He knew that, but all he saw was the money that was going to the lawyers.

My children were three, four, and six years old when their father left. We were married almost ten years and up until the preceding eighteen months, our lives had been exciting, productive, and promising. Each night as his head hit the pillow, he said, "Have I told you today how much I love you?" Even though he would fall into bed exhausted from putting in long hours at our family business, our future looked bright.

It came to our attention that one of our neighbors was openly cheating on his wife, driving his girlfriend by his house while his children were playing in the front yard. Robert was appalled, or so I thought. Ironically, the following year, my formerly faithful husband drove to and from Houston several days a week with his loyal secretary. I was extremely uneasy about the situation, and the first night he didn't come home, our lives took a major shift. I knew we were in big trouble.

Most of our obstacles would melt away if, instead of cowering before them, we should make up our minds to walk boldly through them.[8]

—Orison Swett Marden

There are times, especially during a divorce or child custody battle, when it takes a lot of courage to do the right thing. Divorce is complicated, and many times, our choices aren't so clear. Emotions can block our ability to see reasonably. When we are able to take the emotional aspects out of the situation, we can begin to see more clearly and act more rationally. Apply a clear, objective mind to your interactions with an ex, and you will find that things go more smoothly. Much easier said than done; this is true. You can practice in small ways. When larger issues come up, you will be prepared.

Evaluate the pros and cons of any decision before you proceed. Gather advice from someone you trust. Pray over it. Then stand your ground.

During the divorce proceedings, our young children went with their dad for visitations, which meant they were with "the other woman" as well. This tore me apart. He would drive her sports car to pick up the kids. She came to pick them up from daycare on Friday for their visitation time. They would unplug the phones so the children couldn't phone me when they were with him (I learned this years later). I knew the kids were confused.

I asked my attorney if there wasn't something that could be done to prevent the children from having to spend their visitations in this situation. She was very hesitant to address it in court. I could tell she didn't like the idea of asking a judge about it. She was afraid he might not like it. I remained resolute. So, we decided at the time the temporary orders were established that I could say something to the judge if I still wanted to.

The day came, but so did the voice inside my head, "Just who do I think I am?" I did not want to do this. I fully expected a bad reaction from my husband, knowing how he liked to be the one in control of any situation. I felt discouraged by my attorney, the courtroom, and by what might happen if I spoke my mind. I remember the day. I wore a dress my mother had made. I looked simple, thin, and frail; there was nothing flashy or sexy about me. My negative thoughts were powerful. *Who do you think you are? Why am I the one doing this?* My knees went weak. Standing before a judge can be intimidating (I was easily intimidated in those days). I had lived with a master of intimidation, and I realized that my words spoken to a judge might not make things go in my favor.

I stood before the judge; he looked down from his elevated bench, and I asked, "Is it acceptable for my children to spend the night in the house with my husband and another woman before the divorce is final?" He said without hesitation, "No, it isn't." Then he firmly advised my husband that the children were not to stay with a member of the opposite sex during *his* visitation. It was written into the temporary orders.

Just who did I think I was? I was a mother, hurting and hoping I could make a point that marriage should mean something.

The reaction I had expected did not take long. My husband wrote a letter to the children. Not that they could read it or even begin to understand what he was saying, so I have to believe his words were intended for me. In it, he said, "The judge wants me to lie about my life to you kids, but I know in my heart that I would rather show my love for you by not seeing you than to lie to you about where I live."

So for several, weeks he did not see the children. That resolve didn't last long; he decided out of the blue it was time to have them again. Okay, they are his children, but I soon learned that during visitation, to comply with the court order, they spent the night with the other woman, but their dad left to spend the night elsewhere. He managed to circumvent the court order. After all, wasn't he within the letter of the law? The children were not spending the night with their dad *and* a member of the opposite sex in the same house.

Later, we were in court again for more final orders and I asked the judge if this new arrangement was acceptable according to the court order. I will never forget the look on the judge's face when I explained what was happening. "No," he said emphatically, "it is not acceptable."

The judge did something few people had ever done. He addressed Robert with serious force and made it clear that if he wanted to have visitation with his children without a member of the court present, he would respect the orders of the court.

Much water has passed under the bridge since then. I tell of it here to make one simple point: Sometimes it is necessary to face down the gremlins when they ask you the question, "Just who do you think you are?" If you hear that gremlin sitting on your shoulder, whispering in your ear words that cause you to doubt yourself, face him down. When you hear those words: "Just who do you think you are?" Be ready with an answer.

The truth is we do not need to be perfect before we can set healthy boundaries. We are all imperfect. If you accept this truth, you've taken the first step towards establishing healthy boundaries. I suggest you do an honest evaluation of your situation to learn the source of your problems.

It might be messy, but it is worth the effort. If you are compassionate towards yourself in this process, you will uncover answers as to why you do the things that create problems in your life or don't set the boundaries for your own good. You must find the source of your struggle. It could be as simple as not being taught or disciplined as a child to manage money or plan your time well. It may be a much more complicated issue that you will need a professional counselor to help you with. No matter what, you owe it to yourself to establish healthy boundaries.

Marriage is not the only relationship that requires boundaries. Our friendships can be every bit as emotionally intimate and vulnerable to boundary breakers. In Dr. Jay Carter's book *Nasty People*, he talks about identifying people who are "invalidators—ones who feed on your self-esteem, your self-confidence, your personal worth; ones who cause confusion and uncertainty that is difficult to define; ones who can cause mental anguish; ones who can cause a gnawing unhappiness."[9]

Personality Traits

Play Sanguine - Yellow

The Talker

Talkative - Cheerful - Colorful Clothing
Loud voice - Open life (TMI) - Touchy-feely
Dramatic - Loves to make people laugh
Curios - Wide eyed - Loves attention

Strengths	Struggles
Loves people	Lacks focus
Makes friends easily	Easily distracted
Charming storyteller	Talks too much
Exciting - salesman	Dislikes schedules
Good sense of humor	Looses track of time
Optimistic	Naive

Emotional needs

Attention – Acceptance "As Is"
Approval – Affection = touch

Controls by: Charm

Peaceful Phlegmatic - Green

The Watcher

Quiet -Easy going - Witty sense of humor
Flexible - Light on their feet - Low key
Clothing needs to be comfortable
Steady worker - Peace loving - Kind

Strengths	Struggles
Has few enemies	Stubborn
Steady - Reliable	Dislikes change
Considerate	Hard to get moving
Good listener	Procrastinates
Laid back- easy going	Lies to keep the peace
Gentle	Unmotivated - slow

Emotional needs

Peace & Quite – Feelings of Worth
Lack of stress – Rest = Sleep

Controls by: Procrastination

Powerful Choleric - Red

The Doer

Natural Leader * Decisive * Directional
Likes to get things done * Always on the move
Points finger pointing and pounds fist while talking

Strengths	Struggles
Natural born leader	Overconfident
Usually right	Can't say "I'm sorry"
Loves a Challenge	Quits when they can't win
Problem fixer	Wants to be the boss

Emotional needs

Accomplishment, Support & Loyalty
Sense of Control, Credit for their work

Desire: To make the decisions

Controls By: Angry out bursts

Proper Melancholic - Blue

The Thinker

Private * Proper * Sensitive
Organize their thought using chart and lists
Quiet * Not flashy * Artistic/Musical * Systematic

Strengths	Struggles
Analytical	Perfectionist
Works well alone	Loner
Planner - Organized	Stunted under pressure
Deep thinker	Over sensitive - selfish

Emotional needs

Space to be alone, Silence = No people
Sensitivity to feelings, Understanding

Desire: To follow the rules

Controls by: Moodiness

When you find yourself in a place where you must deal with nasty people, it helps to understand that many of our boundaries are personality based. For example, if you look on the chart for the Proper Melancholic personality type, you will see that one of the emotional needs for this personality type is, "Sensitivity to their feelings," which makes these persons much more susceptible to getting their feelings hurt. So, when a Powerful Choleric, who has the natural tendency to step in and take over, or if a Playful Sanguine, who interrupts people while they are talking, exhibits these natural behaviors to the Proper Melancholic, they get their feelings hurt—boundary breached! Often the Proper Melancholic will think, *They must really dislike me if they treat me with such disrespect.* As though the only time someone would take over, or interrupt is when they dislike the other person. In reality, everyone behaves according to their natural personality "struggles." Obviously, with maturity and a bit of understanding, we can learn to respond to others in a way that makes them feel respected and loved, lessening the number of times our boundaries are breached. After I learned about personality types, dealing with people became much easier.

Most of us have been taught the Golden Rule: "Do unto others as you would have them do unto you." Only that doesn't always work because we all have a different idea of what feels right, i.e., being kind and trusting others to do the same. Unfortunately, this doesn't always work either. Kathryn Robbins, life coach and coauthor of *What Makes You Tick: Self Scoring Adult Personality Assessment Profile*, helps her clients use the personality information to identify the natural strengths, struggles, and emotional needs for each personality type. Being able to identify natural personality behaviors helps take the personal offense out of the irritations that happen in relationships. She suggests we step back and ask, "What emotional need can I meet for the other person—right now?"[10] By stepping back and assessing the situation, the circumstances can shift from a frenzied emotional mess to a proactive relationship.

Doing a personality profile will not pigeonhole you into a box or limit you, but instead, will give you a starting point for understanding natural personality-based behaviors. From there you can work on a personalized maturity plan for yourself and others which in turn helps you build (or rebuild) emotionally healthy relationships.

"Only the weak are cruel. Gentleness can only be expected from the strong."[11]

—Leo Buscaglia

See Appendix II for additional personality resources.

SMORE TO CONSIDER

On a scale of 1 to 10, how do you feel about setting boundaries with people in your private life?

Uncomfortable   Comfortable

1 --- 2 --- 3 --- 4 --- 5 --- 6 --- 7 --- 8 --- 9 --- 10

What do you feel are your internal struggles with boundaries?

Past trauma, mom had poor boundaries.

What area of your life do you feel needs a boundary remodel? Name one thing you can do right now to start that process.

Inspite of the circumstances. I need 2 spk up when things arent right. This pushes back is good for selfesteen.

college - I should have asked someone to get tutor. straight away.

apprenticeship - should have raise with A team D/o even if its on an informal level as suffering in silence hasnt helped, if anything it has exasbated situain.

CHAPTER THREE

Living with Grief

In three words I can sum up everything I've learned about life:
It goes on.[12]

—Robert Frost

Grief is a part of living. When you experience loss, you must find a way to process your emotions through all the stages to the point of acceptance. We all resist change, and death or divorce is the ultimate in change. Grieving a loss of any sort takes time. Grief cannot be rushed; there are no short cuts. Just as life progresses in a natural course over time, so does grief take its course.

Loss of a Loved One

My first extended period of grief came when I lost my father. I was twenty-seven and a new mother. Robert and I moved to Nederland, Texas, in December 1974. Our daughter, Treva, was four months old. We were living in a small rental house on South Sixth Street.

Daddy had not been well for years, but no one knew why. None of the doctors, numerous as they were, knew why Daddy felt ill all the time. He sat in his recliner day in and day out. His skin was a bronze tone even though he never went outdoors. Dad's recent blood work showed his blood sugar was out of control, so my brother, Don, drove him to Houston's Diagnostic Hospital in mid-December. Daddy nearly went into a diabetic coma on the way. He was diagnosed almost immediately with hemochromatosis, a genetic disorder that causes the body to retain iron. He had been sick for many years.

A month after moving to Nederland, I went to have my hair done for the first time since Treva's birth; naturally, I took her with me. I headed home in my second-hand, fixed-up Oldsmobile. When I drove into the driveway, Robert, met me and said bluntly, "Your dad died."

It was hard to believe. Just the day before, I talked with my mother about Daddy's situation. I remember standing in our little den, the yellow phone to my ear, while she told me her concerns about *how* she could or *if* she could take care of him. She felt the disease caused more problems than she could possibly handle on her own. After that conversation, I hung up the phone and prayed, "Lord, whatever is best for everyone, including Daddy, *please*."

I was only able to get to Houston once during the time he was in the hospital, and I didn't think he would die now that we knew what the problem was. I had stitched a crewel embroidered picture of "The Church in the Wildwood" which I gave to my parents during that time, (it now hangs in my laundry room where I can see it from the kitchen). But now, my daddy is dead.

My brother, Don, picked me up to go to the hospital in Houston. We talked only a little during the one-and-a-half-hour trip. Our siblings, Jaynet and Helen, were already there with Mother.

Dr. Gregory met with us in a small alcove. He used medical terminology to explain what had happened, and I snapped. I didn't care if he was considered the "Father of the Medical Center" or not; my daddy was gone. I didn't want to hear a scientific explanation. I wanted to hear Daddy laugh again—that rolling chuckle I loved so much.

He was only sixty-six years old; I was only twenty-seven. We were all too young to say a final goodbye. This kind of grief was something new to me and my heart was broken: for my mother, for my siblings, and for myself. I was his last child, and I had just given birth to my first child, the last grandchild he would see. I felt short-changed. Death came too soon, and the finality shocked me.

Loss of a Relationship

The grief experienced over the loss of a marriage is life altering. It often includes surprises and disappointments no other grief experience can prepare you for.

It was five days before Christmas, the first since my divorce, and the first Christmas I would spend without my children. "Joy to the World" was playing on the car radio, but I did not feel any joy in my world.

My children were born like stair steps, three babies in three years. The older two children were in school by this time, but having to place my youngest in daycare crushed my already broken heart. I was no longer a stay-at-home mom. Being a full-time homemaker had been a whirlwind of diapers, teething, colic, and allergies, but now an additional job working outside the home was a necessity.

During the pre-child part of my life, I had taught theater, but I quickly realized this job option would require evening rehearsals, performances, and weekend competitions—duties which would not be practical with young children. I was college bound once more and became certified to teach English. Just one harsh year after the separation, I was commuting forty minutes to teach in another community. This meant I dressed the children while they were still semi-asleep, (a bit like dressing a rag doll) so that I had enough time to prepare my lunch, drop them off at the sitter, meet a carpool, and arrive at work on time. I felt like I had put in a day's work before I even arrived on the job.

Each evening, there were often stacks of dirty dishes, piles of laundry, children needing help with homework, and my own students' papers to grade. I fell asleep most nights so exhausted I barely tucked the children into their beds with a goodnight kiss, much less a story and time to talk about their day.

All these thoughts whirled in my head as I listened to "Joy to the World." It was Friday, and I was on my way to pay the sitter who was a wonderful woman and a blessing in this hard time. As much as I loved my sitter, my heart was heavy, because this trip home would not be with my children in tow. They would be staying with their dad until the afternoon of Christmas day.

They were so precious to me, and they were at just the ages that made Christmas extra special. Their eager, wide-eyed expectations had made Christmas mornings fun for me the last few years. I was trying hard not to imagine a Christmas morning without their giggles and squeals of delight when they saw the surprises that had mysteriously appeared under the tree overnight.

When I drove my old station wagon onto the babysitter's driveway, a familiar sleek, black sports car parked proudly before me. My heart sank. I knew it was Robert's "lady" friend and not their dad coming to pick up my children. Should I stay or go? Confusion gripped me. Before I could decide to leave, my children came out of the house, climbed into her car and waved, "Bye Mommy," to me as if I was an acquaintance beside the road. And, just like that, they were gone.

I paid the sitter without a word and returned to my car where despair overpowered me. My anxiety grew until all the muscles in my neck and back clinched into knots, and I began to sob. Soon hot tears poured onto the cold steering wheel. How could this be happening? How could I get through Christmas without them? "Oh God, please, please, please get me through this."

As I drove home in a blur, I could hear my mother saying, "In love's service, only the saddened qualify." Well, I certainly must be qualified! I had never known such sadness in all my life. If serving is what qualifies the saddened, then I was willing to serve, in any way it took to remove the pain I was feeling.

"What can I do, God? What can I do?"

Then a wonderful idea hit me! Since I have been involved in theater all my life, I would become a Christmas elf for children who were not as fortunate as my own. It was easy to put together a Christmas elf costume: a green felt skirt, tights, green elf shoes, a green hat made from gift-wrap, and a bit of stage make-up completed the look.

I dialed the number of a local hospital. "Hello, I was wondering if you had children who are still in the hospital, and if they would like a visit from a Christmas elf."

"Yes, we have a few. Are you with a group?"

"No, just me."

"Well, I guess that would be okay," a pause, then, "Yes, come on."

Soon I was on my way to the children's ward in my old station wagon. There were sure to be children there who would welcome a visit from a Christmas elf. I would get to see eyes filled with wonder after all.

An elf's arrival in a hospital, even at Christmas, attracts quite a bit of attention. Heads turned, and some people grinned, but my goal was so intense that my inhibitions had vanished. Children still hospitalized so close to December 25th are either very ill, or their parents are financially unable to provide a Christmas for them and have opted to keep them hospitalized. Either way, they need a boost.

My first stop was to see Larry. "Hi, Larry. How are you doing?" I asked with an elfish grin. His eyes lit up as I walked into his dimly lit room. He did not speak at first. He could not believe his eyes. I handed him a candy cane and a coloring book.

"Say thank you," said an adult voice from the dim corner.

"Thank you," Larry spoke softly.

There were tubes and medical devices all around him, but for those brief moments, there was no pain as fantasy prevailed.

Next, I went to an older boy in the next room.

"Hi, Dale. Merry Christmas! I just came by for a quick visit."

"Are you for real?" he questioned.

"Sure, I am," I replied. "It's Christmas, you know."

I handed him a candy cane. He was alone in the room. Dark circles under his eyes and needles in his frail arms made a clear picture that he would not be leaving the hospital for a while yet. I sat on the edge of his bed and read *How the Grinch Stole Christmas.*

The last child I saw was a girl. She was very unhappy about being in the hospital and made it clear that she did not care for visits from elves at Christmas, or any other time for that matter. She took the candy and seemed pleased that I treated her with respect, even though I was an elf.

"Christmas is really a birthday celebration, you know," I said.

She nodded.

"What is your name?" I asked.

"Tava," she said clearly. "That's Ava with a T in front for Tough."

I could tell she did not really want to be as tough as she thought she needed to be. I held her hand, and she began to relax a little. A faint smile came to her lips.

"Well, Tava," I said, "I hope you will remember to celebrate the birthday party." I left her smiling with an inexpensive little necklace as a gift.

I did not linger long with any of them. I hoped to provide each child with a bit of fantasy to tell their other visitors about, or just to give the children a fond memory. The element of surprise was the best gift. The expression on their faces inspired me too. The spirit of Christmas, the spirit of Christ was coming through. Christmas—the spirit of love in action. It was so exhilarating; I went on to two other hospitals without even calling ahead. Walking in unannounced added to the drama for me, as well as for the nursing staff.

On the way home, I was so wrapped up in my adventure that I forgot about my appearance. There I sat at a traffic light in my old station wagon, which happened to be green, and my green costume with red-painted cheeks and artificial freckles. Without a thought, I glanced over to the other lane and saw a gentleman in a black suit and tie, driving a huge black Lincoln Continental, laughing. I took a moment and looked at myself through his eyes, and realized my pain was gone for the moment, just like my new little hospital friends had experienced. I had completely forgotten my appearance and my sorrow. Christmas was not about me. It was about God's gift to mankind—Jesus the Christ Child. I could go back to my empty house now and plan for the after Christmas celebration. When my children returned, I would have a spirit of true joy in my heart—the joy of Christmas. I had committed to share with others, regardless of my current circumstances, and the joy that was returned to me was far greater than the sorrow that had threatened to overpower me.

Grief can awaken us to new values and new and deeper appreciations. Grief can cause us to reprioritize things in our lives, to recognize what's really important and put it first. Grief can heighten our gratitude as we cease taking the gifts life bestows on us for granted.[13]

—Roger Bertcshausen

According to Debra Warner, MS, MFT, in her article, "7 Steps to Overcome Your Divorce,"

"Divorce is one of the most painful experiences that one can survive. It's often tied to the fear that the pain will never end. The loss a divorce brings has been compared to the stages of death, because the experience is often that of not only losing your marriage but yourself as well. It reaches out and changes everything: the children, family, friends, business associates, and overall community that make up the interwoven support system of the couple."[14]

"Absolutely nobody grieves correctly, according to everybody else."[15]

—Fredda Wasserman

Experts agree that no two people grieve in the same way. As with other types of grief experiences, the death of a marriage is not just a moment in time, but a process or journey that is filled with many different feelings. Grief is not linear! You cannot just pass through the stages of shock, denial, anger, and acceptance in a well-defined order. Divorce, like grief following a death, can be messy and circular, leaving you with the feeling of getting nowhere. The stages of grief change daily or moment-to-moment.

I wish someone had told me this one simple truth—give yourself time to grieve. Don't be too hard on yourself, no matter what others say. They do not like to see people sad, so they may try to fix you or suggest you smile more, hoping it will ease the pain. You are the one going through it. Respect your feelings. Experience them. Work through them. Love and care for yourself.

We know that routines create safe, secure, and predictable environments in times of upheaval. Routines create a sense of control over your turmoil. Routines will help your children feel safe as well. We could all use a greater sense of positive expectation, which is what routines provide. Your routine will guide you as you learn to set limits on your own life.

Here are seven practical and doable tips for transitioning to your new life. Number seven may be the most difficult.

1. Treat yourself gently. At least once a day give yourself permission to do something you enjoy.

    a. Take a warm bath by candlelight.
    b. Polish your nails.
    c. Go window-shopping.
    d. Take a walk.

    The ultimate self care is to create a life you don't need to run from.

2. Stay around positive people. People's words affect us. Brain chemistry changes with our mood.

3. Do something different every day. Cook a new dish. Watch a television program you've not seen before. Take a new route to work.

4. *finance control* Make a list of what you can do now that you couldn't do while in the relationship: Possibilities for your future; personal goals for next week, next month, six months, and for one year ahead; personal dreams.

5. Identify triggers for your grief. Remove photos that upset you. Don't play music that upsets you. Limit conversations about your ex when talking with friends. Go to different places than those you went to with him.

memy 26. Make a plan. Consider an achievable adventure in your personal life. Plan a celebration for the next holiday. Give yourself time, but mark a date on your calendar when you will have made decisions for your future.

7. Do a complete autopsy of your previous relationship and accept that the past is past. You don't have to relive it; you can learn from it.

Life is a journey with choices at every turn. Our choices determine which paths we take. You make numerous choices every day. Give yourself credit for all the healthy choices you make. As mothers, when we feel at ease and confident, our children will pick up on our feelings and mirror them. Above all, stay on the path with the Light (the Lord) at the end.

There are times in every life when heartache tries to overtake us. There is no ache quite like heartache. When you are reminded of sweethearts . . . remember that they are not all "sweet."

As a single woman, you've probably experienced those times. If you can step back and emotionally untangle from your situation, you will lessen the debilitating effects that grief brings. Grief doesn't wait for an invitation; it just comes.

SMORE TO CONSIDER

On a scale of 1 to 10, where would you say your level of emotional grief is right now?

Content   Horrible

1 --- 2 --- 3 --- 4 --- 5 --- 6 --- -7 --- 8 --- 9 --- 10

What is something you can do right now that would be proactive in lessening your grief? (Look at the list of seven doable tips.)

Consistently in morning leve routines, meditation, exercise, read.

How might you handle grief in a healthier way—what things can you stop doing and what thing can you start doing?

Stop looking back, start looking forward and learning from the past make 2morrow better

What kind of "routine" can you put in place right now that will help your children?

If guilt is an issue, what do you feel guilty about and why?

I couldnt do more for Gran. money rules— I could have challenged the authorities.

CHAPTER FOUR

Living with Courage

We must be willing to let go of the life we have planned, so as to have the life that is waiting for us .

—Joseph Campbell

It can be extremely difficult for single women to enter the job market if they have not been employed outside the home before. Sometimes it may seem impossible, but having a job is a necessary part of life. The job interview is a challenging experience in itself.

Landing a job requires a level of confidence that may be damaged by divorce or an abusive marriage. We all know it takes courage to sell yourself and your skills. I recall an early job search of my own. My dad always said when it comes to getting hired, "You have to let them know if they don't hire you, they've made a mistake."

I never had enough nerve to do that until, as a young married woman, I was in need of a job—a real job. There were three ads in the Houston Post that described jobs I thought I could handle. I had never had a "real job" before, one that required forty hours a week and a boss that meant business. This would be the first.

My first interview was for the managerial position for several mall kiosks that sold common greenhouse plants in cute containers. I arrived a little early to the interview. The person who was going to interview me was a young man who wasn't much older than I was. He asked that I take a walk through the greenhouse while he finished some business. As I strolled the aisles, I recalled gardening with my mom. I have adored flowers of every kind since childhood.

The interview began with the usual questions: background, education, job history (something I had precious little of). He began to withdraw saying, "I have two others to interview. I'll let you know." I thought, *I can handle this job, but he isn't going to hire me.* Daddy's words came back to me and out of my mouth. I heard myself say, "If you don't hire me, you're making a mistake."

He was stunned. So was I. He grinned, "What makes you think so?" With confidence, I replied, "Because I know the name of every plant in your greenhouse."

He nodded. His expression more serious now, "You may be right, but I'm obligated to interview the other two applicants."

I had another interview that same day with a different company for a graphic layout artist. At the end of the interview, I said to the man, "I need at least $25 more a month than you are offering." He left the room for a few minutes and returned with a smile. "You've got the job."

My first real job! I had my own work area. What a thrill! 1971 was the start of new beginnings. The real kick came at 7:30 a.m. the next morning when the kiosk manager for the plant kiosk job called to offer me that position.

"I'm sorry," I said, "I've already taken a job."
"I knew it," he said, "I knew you would be hired by now."

Over the years, I've been on several job hunts, most of them as a single mother. I've held many different kinds of jobs and gone through the challenges of interviews and finding the right job in the right place at the right time. After my divorce, I attempted to find a position as a high school theater teacher since that was the area of my degree, skills, and education, but at one interview, a school administrator pointedly asked, "How can you manage this position with all the evening rehearsals and weekend contests as a single mom with three children?" This probably wasn't a legal question, but it was one I needed to consider. How would I juggle directing plays at school and children at home? What was I thinking?

Though my mother was determined to stand by my side and assist in any way she could, I wasn't being realistic to put that kind of pressure on her, no matter how much she loved me. It was a wake-up call.

A school principal in my hometown advised me that in order to be the most employable educator, I needed additional certifications. The more subjects I could teach, the more job security I would have.

As I rounded this turning point, I saw that I would have to learn to be open. Being open to a change or new ideas can be just the thing that works for you in your new situation.

I was able to attend classes for two summer semesters at Lamar University, where I had received my bachelor's degree, and earned a teaching certificate in English. My high school theater teacher recommended me for a job in a school district forty-five minutes away, and I accepted it. Teaching high school English wasn't a dream job, far from it, but it was a start.

When a dream collides with reality, reality seldom falls to its knees.
—Unknown

Letting go of the idea that we shouldn't settle for less than our dream occupation may be difficult. So often, our dreams become our identity, but we must be open to learning something new. Sometimes these side steps open doors that we would never think to knock on but which may be just what we're looking for.

The workforce is always shifting; new ways of living produce new ways of doing things—and new jobs. You may find yourself in a state of inertia. Change is the single thing we humans resist more than anything else. It would be so much easier to do what we are accustomed to doing, the familiar. Change happens and those who are willing to adjust are the ones who move forward.

After I taught for a few years, I realized my salary would not increase significantly unless I had a master's degree. The only avenue for higher income as a teacher is to have a higher-level degree. When my children were nine, seven, and six years old, I made the decision to return to college.

Earning a master's degree seemed like an adventure. However, the thought of moving three children to another city, locating day care and a place to live for three months in the summer, and paying for it all was an overwhelming leap of faith, so I took one baby step at a time.

The process was not all smooth travels. For acceptance into graduate school, I had to take the Graduate Records Exam (GRE). I had not taken a standardized test in eighteen years. I also would need three open slots in a daycare for the summer months in a city where the openings were few. I took baby steps of faith.

I prepared for the GRE, but even so, it was no easy feat. When I received the results, I had mixed feelings. I had scored fairly well on all three sections. The trouble was they only counted two of the three, and I didn't quite make the cut for automatic admission to the graduate school at The University of Texas at Austin. This meant I'd have to gather letters of recommendation, transcripts, fill out more forms, and meet with the dean in order to be accepted on probation. This required swallowing my pride.

I could have given up at that point. I could've said, "Maybe this isn't meant to be." My desire to prove the test wrong was as strong as my desire to achieve something that would change my life. I had a brief meeting with the dean as a formality. He nodded, signed a paper, and I was accepted. It was the first inkling that determination is a big part of reaching a goal.

I still would have to make arrangements for the care of three children while I was in class. Most openings in the nice childcare centers were not available just for the summer. Friends told me, "Parents pay for spots to hold them even if they aren't using them in the summer."

The university had an office for returning students that gave me a list of 100 childcare centers in the city. They had everything from tiny home-based centers to large ones. There were centers that focused on horseback riding, computers, and some focused on nothing at all. I drove by several and called others. I wasn't having any luck until the day I visited St. Martin's Lutheran in downtown Austin. My thinking was that it would be too expensive and certainly wouldn't have a decent playground located in the heart of the city as it was.

The elderly director cordially welcomed me and gave me a complete tour. She pointed out that the new playground had been given an award and then asked, "May I sign up your children?" Stunned I asked, "You know I have three children?" She said she did, and I was able to enroll all three in one of the highest quality daycares in Austin. The last piece in the puzzle was housing. It was too late to qualify for university housing and at the moment, I lived too far away to do the research on my own, so Carliss, a lifelong friend, who lived in Austin, began to search for me. Time was running out. I had a deadline for getting any of the down payments for tuition and childcare back, and it was approaching quickly. We had posted on bulletin boards in every place Carliss could think of. Shortly before the last week to back out, she called, "I've found an apartment that you can sublet. It is in a quaint complex in the Clarksville area of Austin. You can lease it for the summer." It was going to happen. But how would I manage the day-to-day routine and all the changes for the kids?

The shuttle bus system runs like a spider-web across the city with stops all over the university campus. Imagine my surprise when I learned the bus stopped at the corner near our apartment and drove directly to the corner of St. Martin's Lutheran. I could choose either of two buses from the daycare center that would stop in the front of the education building where all my classes took place. This was truly amazing, considering the size of The University of Texas at Austin.

The odds of my figuring all that out and making it happen in my own power were slim, but one baby step at a time taken in faith blazed the trail and prepared the way for me.

After three summers, on our final trek home my children put a poster on the back of our station wagon: "Hurray, hurray. We're happy as can be. Mom just finished at UT."

"We gain strength, and courage, and confidence by each experience in which we really stop to look fear in the face . . . we must do that which we think we cannot."[16]

—Eleanor Roosevelt

Facing the job market for the first time or after being out of the workforce for a while requires more than a bit of courage. Most women who are full-time homemakers and mothers do not give themselves credit for the managerial skills and knowledge they have acquired and use daily—twenty-four, seven. Homemakers use workplace skills all the time. For example: meal planning, scheduling activities, paying bills, and balancing a budget. All these skills will be valuable in the workplace. You may find that in a crisis you are more willing or even pushed to test your limits. You may be surprised at what you can do.

Even if change is difficult for you, take a moment and consider a few of the opportunities open to you. Many of the things we feel are just dreams are obtainable with a bit of planning and the courage to try.

You may find your next step requires more education. Before rejecting the idea of returning to school, talk to an advisor or coach and see what kind of doors open for you. Education is something that can never be taken away from us. It is about more than the knowledge you gain in a classroom. It is about expanding your reach, being exposed to new ideas, and experiencing self-awareness and building self-esteem. It is about the journey. Along the way many single moms, just like you, achieve a stronger awareness of their self-worth.

You are not alone. There are many women traveling the same path who are on their own. All of them are heading towards their distinct destinations. You are on the path to your future—one that is right for you.

Always continue the climb. It is possible for you to do whatever you choose, if you first get to know who you are and are willing to work with a power that is greater than ourselves to do it.[17]

—Ella Wheeler Wilcox

SMORE TO CONSIDER

After reading the chapter on job hunting and courage, what do you feel are your options for work?

List three jobs you would consider "dream jobs." List two reasons you feel they qualify to be dream jobs.

1. _L+D_
   a. _live + breame in aumute._
   b. _LD. people gump._
2. _consumancy_
   a.
   b.
3.
   a.
   b.

What frightens you most about job hunting?
overmelming, a job to get a job.

Do you have a current resume written?

[ ] Yes [✓] No

If you knew nothing could go wrong, what would you attempt? What leap of faith do you need to take?

Put myself out mue more. Promo.

CHAPTER FIVE

Learning to Be Self Aware

Caterpillar asks, 'Who are YOU?' to which Alice replies she no longer really knows anymore, after all the recent changes.

—Lewis Carroll, *Alice in Wonderland*

No matter how you feel about your life, you are not in Alice's wonderland where time is suspended. You could feel dazed by the endless list of duties that you trudge through day after day. Time passes, children grow, and you realize you merely exist through it all. Perhaps you are bewildered or hurting—anxious or confused; there may be times when you feel like Alice, wishing you could shrink yourself in order to hide from the overwhelming responsibilities you face. You may think your life is absurd, wondering as Alice did, if you are the same person that you were yesterday, but I'm here to tell you, you are not losing your senses. Your divorce, the death of your spouse, or coping with a husband who is away a large part of the time for his job, such as for military service or sales, has left you wondering if you are the same person you used to be. No matter how you became single or almost single, you have now stepped into the complicated world of motherhood without a spouse or partner.

As Alice put it, "I don't feel like *me* anymore. I wonder if I'm somebody else after all." Have you ever felt like Alice, wondering who you actually are? You may have delayed or denied your dreams to be a wife and mother, or quit your job to be a homemaker. In so doing, you made a sacrificial choice. However, your personality's emotional needs may have suffered. When our emotional needs go unfulfilled, often resentment results, and sometimes dysfunctional behavior starts taking over our ability to think straight, causing all kinds of craziness. If you, like Alice, are wondering if you are indeed yourself, or maybe you've never known who your true self is, a look at your God-Given Personality Style (G.P.S.) can help you navigate out of the strangeness of this Wonderland. It's amazing how easy it is to lose yourself, and how hard it is to find you again, but don't lose hope, it can be done.

Make it thy business to know thyself, which is the most difficult lesson in the world.[18]

—Miguel de Cervantes

Growing up in a home where compliments were rare, I yearned for the recognition I received from audiences. I treasured the acting trophies I received during high school, but I would have treasured acknowledgement from my parents more. I did not receive their praise. Their generation avoided vanity at all costs. They were proud of that.

As a freshman at Lon Morris College, I joined the theater group, anticipating the same applause I received in high school, only that wasn't the case. I turned out to be more of a little fish in a big pond.

Our college wasn't large, in size or numbers, but the theater department was known for its outstanding talent, and I found myself surrounded by students who already had experience on professional stages in Houston. I had been a shining star in my hometown, but now bigger stars eclipsed my "shine."

Being the new kid on the block, I desired to be part of the action, so I worked after hours as a seamstress in the theater department to cover a portion of my tuition. When the theater director discovered what a competent seamstress I was, I worked all day on Saturdays as well as putting in time on other days, appliquéing patches on costumes for the show *Lil Abner*. I learned later the costumes were so well made the college rented them to other theaters.

I had become the small "sewing" fish in the pond of larger, more colorful fish. It's no wonder I returned home after my freshman year with my little light almost burned out. I had no sense of direction or idea of the path I was to take or the part I was to play. I was living by default, not knowing who I was, what I wanted to do, or where I wanted to go. I was without a compass; I just lived life as it came, adjusting to whatever or whoever was the strongest force at the time.

Dad didn't care for theater. He equated it with Hollywood and Hollywood with immorality. Robert thought my theatrical friends were "weird." It was okay for me to teach drama, but since being an actor was not supported by either my dad or my husband, I gave it up and became a teacher instead, consoling myself with the thought that life can't always be fun or fulfilling. I lived to please others. I altered myself after I married to become the wife, I thought I ought to be, but after ten years of marriage I was finding that wasn't working out very well either.

I remember the day I had to break the news to my mother. "Let's sit down, Mom," I said thinking of how I could share my awful news. We sat on the sofa that Robert and I had bought at a discount warehouse at a low price because two legs were broken off. He was handy and replaced them easily. I loved the old overstuffed sectional that had filled our den in the old house on the outskirts of Houston. It was perfect as far as I was concerned now in the dream home we had designed and built together. Life seemed good: three healthy children and a promising future in my family's business.

I sat staring at the hearth. I finally got the words out, "Robert left." My mind wandered back to the day he had sorted the stones for the fireplace and assembled them carefully in order to stack, place, and set each one for the rustic fireplace I wanted. He was highly capable with his hands. He could build and repair things, refurbish cars, and solve household problems. He took on challenges with gusto, but apparently, the problems in our marriage were beyond what he felt he could fix, so he left.

A lump had taken up residence in my throat. It had been a few days since he had gone. Since my father's passing five years earlier, my mother and I had become closer. We lived in the same town, the community where I grew up, which made it all the harder to tell her my bad news.

She tried to encourage me. "You have done all anyone could do," she said, hoping to make me feel better. She knew how hard I had worked to take care of three babies and make our house a home. I had made myself into the perfect homemaker. I had left behind my personal identity to become what I thought my husband wanted.

Mother was right. I had tried to do all the right things. I was functioning as I thought I was supposed to. I was not aware of the mask that had slowly grown like moss on a tree trunk to cover my true personality; the true me had withered in the process. It would be years before I realized the crippling power a personality mask creates.

Mom rarely cried, and she didn't cry now, not in front of me. Mother was the stoic sort. She was practical and hard working. I wouldn't know for many years just how hard our divorce was for her. I learned much later from my older, and only, brother that she had vowed, "I will be there for Gail. Whatever it takes, I will be there for her and her children." And, she was. At the time I was consumed with grief, so I wasn't aware just how hurt my mother and siblings were.

My little family was crumbling, and I couldn't stop it. My world was like an elaborate sandcastle. I could see the waves approaching and knew nothing I could do would hold back the incoming tide. As weeks passed into dreadful months, there were more waves, tidal surges: one deception followed by another disappointment. The children were confused. I was sinking into the sifting sand beneath my feet. I never smiled or laughed. Pain etched my face.

I dared not contemplate the years ahead. I shed a bucket load of tears. Sometimes I broke into sobs watching a television commercial of a happy couple. I went into a depression on holidays. I became terribly self-conscious and felt less than adequate in most situations. Attempts at a social life felt awkward and stilted. Life was made more difficult because I'd lost my true self in a ten-year marriage.

Everything in life had changed for me and the children. There was no way around it. I had to work full-time. The older two were in school. My youngest was in all-day childcare, which he hated.

For the first time in a long time, all the responsibilities for our home fell on my overloaded shoulders. I had to light the furnace in the attic. I managed all the household bills, lawn care, automobile maintenance, and insurance. I made all the decisions including setting personal boundaries.

As I steadily created a life of new routines, new friends, and regular worship and prayer, ever so gradually tiny spaces in my soul began to expand to hold more faith than I'd ever known. The truth is I never before needed so desperately to draw on my faith as at this time.

I discovered it was okay to ask others for help when I couldn't do something such as changing a tire. I also learned I could return to the local university to acquire a teaching certificate in English. I enrolled my children in the day care on campus. I managed a major move, put furniture into storage, and moved us into a rental house. The children and I tackled the changes together, as much as is possible with young children.

I grew spiritually; my mask no longer fit, and slowly the edges curled back and I could see the deep impressions that wearing it had left on my life. I also got a glimpse of the person underneath. I was growing now and these growing pains were uncomfortable.

In the book, *Your Personality Tree*, by Florence Littauer, she talks about taking off the masks we developed for self-preservation and seeing ourselves as God originally intended us to be. By doing so, we are free to spread out our roots and grow.

Many people are playing roles they never auditioned for, on stages they didn't design, while wearing masks they don't know how to remove.[19]

—Florence Littauer

Personality is the term commonly accepted to describe the way we define our human uniqueness. God designed us as matchless. You are "fearfully and wonderfully made" (Ps 139:14, NIV). Your personality style indicates your consistent patterns of behavior. Your personality traits are motivating factors that influence your decision-making. Faced with similar situations, single parents will make decisions determined by their own personality styles. If you find yourself making choices and then wondering why, your personality profile may reveal insightful clues. Then you can discern if you are making choices that are true to who you were meant to be.

Knowing your God-given personality style brings self-awareness and with it, freedom. This requires an honest look in the mirror. It is crucial to truthfully acknowledge and accept your personality before you embark on your life path. You may find personality profiles online.

"An honest answer, is like a warm hug" (Prov. 24:26, The Message). Hug yourself and bring out your genuine beauty by discovering your authentic strengths, struggles, and emotional needs. By openly and truthfully answering the questions on the profile, you can gain a new sense of self or be reintroduced to the person you once were.

Just as with *Alice in Wonderland*, once you wake-up, you will have a renewed sense of purpose and direction. You will come out of the "rabbit hole" and follow the path that will lead to the freedom of being you. It is okay to let your light shine, to imagine a life filled with hope, to move forward one day at a time, one step at a time if need be.

There's a children's song that we sing that goes like this: "This little light of mine, I'm gonna let it shine." But unfortunately, life can dim our light and we need to learn *how* to let it shine again.

When we embrace our true personality, our light has a chance to do just that—*shine!*

Janet Davis says in *The Feminine Soul*, "In Christian circles, we sometimes hesitate to speak confidently about the wisdom of God within, wrongly equating self-doubt with humility. Could it be that Lady Wisdom (Proverbs 31) is inviting us to a new, bold awareness?"[20] Could it be that you've allowed circumstances to tear you down?

Some women consider difficulties as if life has been cruel to them and something has gone terribly wrong. They think of themselves as victims. Others manage to see difficulties as challenges to be overcome. It is important to accept that life is a series of events that are often troublesome, and it is hard to cope with them. It isn't easy, but keep in mind, easy never propelled anyone into a growth pattern.

In *The Adversity Advantage*, Dr. Paul G. Stoltz says, "Adversity happens. It doesn't play favorites, and it comes in all shapes and sizes. Pain, fear, discomfort, and injustice are far more powerful motivators than their opposites."[21]

Eric Weihenmayer, the world's leading blind athlete and the only blind person in history to scale the Seven Summits (the highest mountains of each of the seven continents), says: *Let adversity be the flame in which your strengths are forged. . . Use adversity to help you grow entirely new strengths and sharpen existing ones . . . Confront the brutal truth about what you currently are and are not good at in the face of your highest aspirations.*[22]

—Eric Weihenmayer, *The Adversity Advantage*

Respect your built-in personality strengths and talents and develop them. In the beginning of my journey, I could no more imagine my future self being full of strength and vitality than the tiny acorn can imagine itself as the mighty oak. I had to trust the process. Our weakness gives others an opportunity for service and increases our humility. Members of a small church group I attended after my divorce donated a Saturday to helping me prepare our house for sale. Between my work, commute, juggling children, and trying to make sense of my life, I just didn't have the energy to get the house ready for the market. They painted doors, cleaned floors, and had gardeners clean up the yard.

As you begin your personal journey, consider the idea that you may have masked your true personality by learning behaviors that are not really you. Women, who are escaping an abusive relationship, often cover over their natural tendencies and become pleasers. It's important to get reacquainted with your true nature in order to become free to be yourself. Some women feel such shame that they do not want to acknowledge their good personality traits. Though it is part of life to want to please others, becoming a "people pleaser" usually doesn't work out well for anyone.

Since discovering my personality type's natural behaviors, I have been able to focus on building my strengths instead of always managing my struggles. Knowing your personality type will open doors to self-awareness. The way you respond to life's events is primarily determined by your natural built-in personality type and followed up by learned behaviors.

- Are you a socialite-party lover, or comfortable being the center of attention?

- Do you only feel at ease when everything in your environment is in its proper place?

- Are you usually the one in charge, the natural born leader who likes to be in charge of things?

- Are you perhaps simply relaxed and easy-going?

Whatever type you are has a significant effect on how you cope with life's difficulties and how you make decisions. When you complete a personality assessment, you will discover both your strengths and your weaknesses—we all have them—strengths and weaknesses.

Every mom who does this will benefit and so will her family. It is easy to think only of your weaknesses, but it is your strengths that will sustain you, and concentrating on your strengths will turn your life around. If you will acknowledge your strengths and downplay your weaknesses, you will discover a clear image of yourself and how you act, react, and interact with others. By concentrating on your strengths, they will increase and grow stronger.

The goal is to identify, accept, and highlight your strengths. According to Marcus Buckingham and Dr. Donald O. Clifton, the authors of *Now Discover Your Strengths*, "You need to become an expert at finding, describing, applying, practicing, and refining your strengths. Suspend whatever interest you may have in weakness and instead explore the intricate details of your strengths."[23]

When I found myself divorced with three young children, I was terrified. I yearned for simple answers to help make decisions. During the years following my divorce, my strengths were forced into action. They were stretched, exercised, and developed. I was fully aware of my weaknesses. They glared me in the face, but it was my strengths that kept me going. I was able to take on challenges, meet new experiences head-on, and enjoy life.

After my divorce, I had another chance to let my joy come out. Expressing myself became a passion for me, and my personality reinforced this. You must understand your true nature before you can develop your strengths so they work in your favor.

"Nothing is so strong as gentleness. Nothing is so gentle as real strength."[24]

—Frances De Sales

SMORE TO CONSIDER

Have you filled out a personality assessment yet?

If not, I encourage you to get one of Florence and Marita Littauer's books. They include personality profiles.

If yes, what category did the profile indicate you might be? What are some adjectives for your category?

What did you learn about yourself?

Name a time of grief when you found you were stronger than you thought you were. Why do you think this was?

Identify your three most significant strengths.
1. *communicating, interpersonal + influencing*
2. *innative*
3. *strong team player*

Identify your three most significant struggles.
1. *boundaries*
2. *self esteem*
3. *self belief*

CHAPTER SIX

Learning to Prioritize

Money isn't the most important thing in life, but it's reasonably close to oxygen on the "gotta have it" scale.

—Zig Ziglar, *Follow Your Dreams*

Of course, money matters, but it seems to matter most when you think it is all that matters. If you have a shift in your household budget due to a divorce, loss of a job, or death of a spouse, you will have to realign your thinking about money. Money will not make you happy all on its own. There are people who are perfectly happy with very little money while others with loads of money are unhappy. It is a matter of perspective.

One of the most important lessons that a lack of money can help us learn is the difference between needing and wanting something. A young mother with two daughters, who had been single for seven years at the time, shared this key lesson with me, "You must keep your focus." She said that she repeatedly taught her girls the difference between needing and wanting. She didn't just bark, "You don't need that," she sat down with them and explained the difference between wanting and needing. She was a wise woman because she knew that sometimes it's easier to show your children the difference between needing and wanting than just explaining it to them. Even though she struggled to make ends meet, she found the time and the giving spirit to do community service and shared that experience with her girls by having them participate with her. It became a family tradition during the Thanksgiving and Christmas holidays to volunteer their time feeding the homeless or delivering meal packages to shut-ins. It was their way of giving back for the times people had helped them. Her children could see with their own eyes what real need was, so when the topic of, "I need a new ____" came up at their home, all she had to say was, "Is it a need or a want?" and the girls knew what she was talking about. By learning to focus, they understood the difference between a need and a want.

The next time you think you need something, ask yourself, "Is it a need or a want?" Most likely, you already know the answer, but it helps to ask.

After determining if it's a need or a want, you'll have to figure out where the money will come from. This is where a budget will help. Perhaps you've never used a budget, but if not, I can assure you that learning to appreciate the power it gives will help to overcome or ward off tough times. It lets you know where you stand. A budget helps keep you focused.

The simplest budget to learn is living by "cash only." This eliminates the temptation of over spending, because when the money is gone—it's gone. Dave Ramsey's envelope system is easy to use and has huge benefits for the beginning budgeter. Ramsey suggests that you divide each paycheck into categories, setting aside the bills that need to be paid by check or bank bill pay from the other expenses that can be paid by cash. Categories such as food, clothing, and entertainment will need to have the allotted cash set aside in an envelope for that month or pay period.

As part of the budget training process in this system, no credit cards are used, no matter what, and no debit cards are used other than to pay a monthly bill instead of writing a check. Shopping is done on a cash only basis—not using cards of either kind. If you have credit cards, your payments to those cards will be part of the budget, but their use is now off limits. Living by cash helps the budgeter stay within her financial means, even if it is limited. This process helps make the needs versus wants decisions much easier to make. To find out more about this simple system and apps for budgeting, visit Ramsey Solutions at: https://www.ramseysolutions.com.

No matter what kind of budgeting system you choose to use, there are a few basic things to take into consideration. Make a list of your financial priorities. Rent or house payment might be at the top of the list, followed by food, utilities, car payment, credit card debt, clothing, school loans, entertainment, etc. Include some treats, such as a massage, a manicure, or a short vacation every so often.

Review and research your financial commitments and spending habits for each month. Break them into categories, using the same categories each month.

Plan ahead for expenditures like back-to-school supplies, birthdays, and Christmas. Have a special savings category for these items.

Develop a savings plan for retirement, even if in tiny amounts. Check to see if your employer does matching funds for a 401K.

Develop a short (1 year) and a longer (5 year) financial plan. What is it that you want to accomplish in one to five years? This can be to buy a newer car, or a house, or to take a trip.

Make contact with someone who can help you. Even Olympic gold medal winners have coaches, so don't feel you need to do this on your own.

"Most of the luxuries and many of the so-called comforts of life are not only not indispensable, but positive hindrances to the elevation of mankind."[25]

—Henry David Thoreau

In every budget there are places where we can trim the fat, so to speak. Our budget often takes a hit at the grocery store. We all must eat—hopefully every day. It is a myth that eating healthy is expensive. Not eating healthy can have its expensive side too. The doctor and dental bills that result from eating junk foods will add up over time. Planning is the best way to stretch your grocery spending. Here are some thoughts regarding budgeting from a single mom's point of view.

- Plan meals based on the money you know you will have.
- Jot down simple menus for the month on a calendar and post it in the kitchen.
- Use the grocery fliers and any coupons for items you would buy, anyway.
- Go grocery shopping as seldom as possible and use your calendar menus to determine what you purchase.
- Allow children to choose a favorite meal and have them help you prepare it. It is a great learning experience for them.

Some restaurant chains have family specials on certain days of the week in which kids eat free during specified hours. As a treat, build that into your calendar. Avoid the impulse to order pizza delivery too often or better yet, make your own.

It's not only the grocery store spending that can kill your budget, but clothing store expenditures can be a super temptation for overspending. Choices about clothes depend on the age of your children. For the most part, young children are not interested in impressing others with their fashion. During those years resist the temptation to buy cute and expensive clothes. Go to resale or thrift shops instead. While you're there, you can drop off any outgrown clothing, either as a donation or for resale on consignment. You may make a few dollars in the process.

Teenagers are self-conscious and their wardrobes mean a lot to them. There are ways to stay in style and not wreck your budget. Be alert to what each child likes and shop carefully. Here's where the envelope system works well: if there isn't any money left in your envelope, you have to put the item back on the rack, which helps you stay within your budget. If you have a teen who will "just die" if they don't have an article of clothing they want, you can give them the opportunity to pay part of the cost. This gives them "ownership" of the purchase and the outcome could have a twofold benefit; they may take better care of their clothing, and it builds self-esteem when they know they are capable of taking care of their own needs or wants.

Childcare may be one of your largest expenses. In most areas, you can find subsidies or discounts. You have to do some research. You may want to visit the Child Care Aware website for valuable resources on finding day care providers. You can also make calls to local agencies and churches in your area, or ask neighbors and friends. Always be cautious. Ask for referrals before leaving your child with someone.

Christmas may be the most stressful time of the year for single mothers. Just like mothers everywhere, single moms want to hear their children squeal with delight on Christmas morning. Children love the surprises of Christmas. When I talk with adults about Christmas, they say it's a moment in their lives when they knew for sure someone did or didn't care for them.

Christmas is a great time to teach children the value of giving. As a child, I once gave away a doll at Christmas to a child in the neighborhood, and that memory of her delight has stayed with me all through the years.

Even with limited means, you can create family traditions, which will carry children through tough times as they grow into adulthood. One of my treasured friends always served tiny sausages, along with other treats from her country of birth, for breakfast on Christmas morning. Although this wasn't extravagant, it was considered a treat in their home. compound Immediately after Christmas is the best time to join a Christmas savings club at your bank. The year I did this was the first time Christmas didn't destroy our budget, even though the amount I put in each time was small.

One single mom told me she put a small amount from every paycheck in a savings account that she opened at a bank other than the one where she regularly banked, so she would be less likely to access it. Sometimes it was only $5.00, but she made a habit of saving.

When money is tight, and you've stretched every penny to its breaking point, the only other solution is to make more money. Here are a few suggestions for increasing your income if only in small amounts. Consider your skills.

- Are you crafty? You could make items to sell at a craft fair, online, Facebook Marketplace, or to individuals you work with. One Christmas, I painted sweatshirts. For more information about starting an arts and crafts business visit https://www.liveabout.com/arts-and-crafts-4688173

- Do you like caring for animals? People are always looking for caring, reliable dog/cat/bird sitters. Ask a veterinarian's office if they will post a flyer for you. Print cheap business cards and post everywhere possible or create a simple website. Weebly offers free sites. Be sure to check out the pros and cons of pet sitting before spending any money on advertising.

- Are you good at decorating Christmas trees? Many people, especially seniors, will gladly pay for this chore. You can also hire out to remove, pack, and put away the decorations.

- Are you good with kids? Many moms need after school care at a reasonable price. Network with your local PTA. Again, know the rules and laws of childcare before advertising.

- Are you a teacher? You could tutor students in your subject of certification, and even if you aren't certified, you could tutor in a subject that you excel in, such as math, or English as a Second Language (ESL).

- Do you sew? Simple alterations could be done after hours and offer a much-needed skill. Leave cards at all your local dry cleaners, or if you feel your skills are up to it, all bridal shops need seamstresses, but keep in mind, you may have to work in their shop. You could make dance costumes for local dance recitals. Think of all the moms who would appreciate this service. Sewing on Boy Scout badges can also make some pocket change.

- Are you a whiz with a computer or email? Offer your skills to the elderly who may want to learn how to use their computers to correspond with their families. Or, offer the service of retyping out-of-print books for authors who may not have a digital copy of their out-of-print book(s).

- If you have a full-time job and still you have more month than money, a second job may be necessary. When my son was a teen, he came back to live with me after having lived with his dad for a while. I had to work part-time in the evenings as a tutor, and he worked at a pizza restaurant. It was necessary and brought in the extra income needed.

NOTHING IS PERM.

Every situation is different. Whatever your situation, a good plan is essential to financial security. If you do not have a job or a steady income, you may think a budget is the least of your concerns. You may not be in the position to consider paying off debts or saving for the future because you are financially dependent on others. Perhaps you are on welfare and food stamps. There are times when it is not only necessary to apply for assistance, but it is the only choice you have. It is certainly not shameful, especially if it is a temporary situation, but you will always have to manage whatever money you have to its fullest extent, so learning to budget will still be valuable. Budgeting not only helps take a bit of stress off your monthly obligations, but it can free you up to dream of bigger and better things for your future.

My friend Stephanie, also divorced, was thrilled to show me her new house. She and I, both single mothers, shared a lot in common, but I hadn't dreamed of buying a house on my own—until then. Her house was all new, brick, and in a nice development. For the first time since the divorce, I began to think about the possibility of owning my own home. How in the world could I finance a house? It was beyond me at that point. Since the divorce several years before, we had to live with Mom until I could rent a house. It made sense not to pay rent if I could purchase a house. The wheels were turning in my head.

The following week I brought up the subject with my fellow teachers. "I want a place with trees and character," I shared.

"You should buy Deena Wood's house," one of my teacher friends suggested. Deena worked at the high school, and I knew where she lived.

"I didn't know it was for sale."

Deena lived in a cottage style home, which just happened to be steps away from the home where I grew up and where my mother still lived. A small park separated my mother's house and Deena's. There were large oak trees in the front and back yards. The location would be perfect.

What was I thinking? I couldn't afford a house. This whole idea was so new to me. That night my curiosity got the best of me and I called, anyway.

Deena's husband, Harry, answered the phone. "Hi, this is Gail Cawley-Parks," he didn't know me by my married name. "I heard that your house is for sale."

"Yes, it is," he replied in a businesslike tone.

"Can you tell me about it?" I was almost embarrassed to ask.

He explained that they had done some remodeling and had added a master suite as well as extending the kitchen.

I finally took a breath and asked, "And what are you asking for it?"

He gave me the price and my heart sank. "That's what I thought it might be. I'm sure it is worth that, but it is more than I can afford, but thanks anyway." I hung up the phone and the reality of purchasing a home set in. How did I think I could buy a house? That was a silly dream.

Just a few minutes later the phone rang. This was long before caller I.D., so I didn't know who it was.

"Gail, this is Harry Wood. Deena and I talked about it and decided for you we will sell the house for. . ." and he gave a figure ten thousand dollars less than the previous price he had given me just minutes before.

Choking back tears of joy, I said, "Oh, my. Really?"

"Yes," he assured me.

"Perhaps I can manage that," I said, almost unable to speak.

I went to see the inside of the house the following day. It was not new, but definitely had character and room for my family.

Ultimately, with a little help from Mom for the down payment and a loan for new first-time homebuyers, I was able to purchase a house. In the years that followed it proved to be the perfect location. My mother could walk over, and she was always available for the kids. They developed a strong bond with her. Each child could get to the campus of their school on a bike. The high school where I worked was right around the corner. Sometimes it's easier to see God's hand than at other times. This time it was easy.

I wish I could say all my financial troubles ended so nicely. They didn't. I worked on budgeting and planning regularly. I made charts. I set goals. On some weekends, I worked with the drama groups for a small stipend. My children and I wore hand-me-downs. I accepted furniture and other items people offered. Money was always in short supply. I was paid monthly, so I had to plan extra carefully. I planned meals a month in advance on a simple calendar on the kitchen wall.

Because, I had learned to budget, when the refrigerator compressor went out, I was able to take advantage of a great deal on another one. We lived within our means, barely, but we did it, which is a healthy source of pride for me.

Money management differs for each of us, but there is one constant that remains: if you aren't making ends meet, you either need to make more money or spend less. Maintaining a positive upbeat attitude is helpful, but this doesn't mean you can spend more than you make and expect miracles to happen every month. Planning and asking for assistance when necessary are the wisest things to do.

SMORE TO CONSIDER

Have you ever created a budget before?

[ ] Yes[ ] No

Why or why not?

Do you have a list of all your bills and expenditures?

[ ] Yes[ ] No

Are you willing to make one?

[ ] Yes[ ] No

Would you be willing to use Dave Ramsey's envelope method of budgeting?

[ ] Yes[ ] No

What goal or project would you like to accomplish for the upcoming year? (This can be getting a GED, upgrading your car, buying an iPad, etc.)

invest £500.

What skills do you have that could be used for generating income?

coaching | mentoring.

What would you like to accomplish in five years?

L+D consultant / coaching

Do you think you would like help figuring out all of this?

[ ] Yes[ ] No

CHAPTER SEVEN

Learning to Wait

I know you can get lonely. I know you can crave companionship and sex and love so badly that it physically hurts. But I truly believe that the only way you can find out that there's something better out there is to first believe there's something better out there. What other choice is there?[26]

—Greg Behrendt, *He's Just Not That Into You*

How can you know if the relationship you are in is love? Do greeting cards, candy, and flowers demonstrate real love? Does saying "I love you," make it real? Love is not only a noun, but it is a verb, an action, reaching past the uncomfortable parts, the daily grind, the boring day, and bringing with it kindness, understanding, forgiveness, and willingness to serve, for no other reason than love. I learned about unconditional love mostly from my mother. Not that she ever said much about it, she simply lived it. She was love in action. Romantic love, though different from the love of a mother, should also stretch itself past the flowers and chocolates and into action.

If human love does not carry a man beyond himself, it is not love.[27]
—Oswald Chambers

I was a single mother for sixteen years. I won't say it was easy or that things always went well during those waiting years. However, I still remember clearly my grown and married daughter, Treva, repeating to me something I had often told her, "Good things come to those who wait."

I didn't learn much about life planning and waiting as a young woman. I liked being married, being a wife, and a mother. It wasn't easy removing my first wedding band. Symbolically my life was as vulnerable as my bare finger. A pale indent remained around my finger where the custom-made ring had been. I desired to have a sense of power over anything in my messed-up life, so I had my ring melted down and remolded into a dinner ring. Tears were just below the surface as my heart melted along with it.

Surely there would be another husband for me, I thought, but no one came along. So, I waited. I'd often watch with envy as others dated and sometimes remarried. At the ballpark, I cheered for my kids alongside other moms and dads who went home together as a couple. Going out was terribly awkward. No man seemed to be a match. So, I waited.

While I waited, I decided to focus more on self-improvement, so I went back to college for a master's degree where all my skills were put to the test. I gained much more than a degree. My self-confidence soared. My children and I created new adventures. My salary increased. Eventually I became a more appealing woman. By being my best self, I attracted men who were also functioning at their best.

Never view waiting as wasted time, these are simply opportune moments allotted for the purpose of regaining some inner stillness, calm and clarity.[28]

—Michele Howe

Accepting your humanness and living your life boldly may bring you into conflict with your upbringing or your religious community. It's not uncommon for people in Christian singles circles to tell women to, "Make a list of all the things you want in a husband and pray over it." Leaders assure them that God will honor their prayers if they do this. I do not know which of the scriptures they use to substantiate this idea, but they firmly believe it. I didn't see the manipulation in this thinking, so I made my list.

My man would:

- Attend church with me
- Not have abandoned his wife and children
- Adore my children as if they were his own
- Be as comfortable and attractive in a suit as in jeans
- Be smarter than I am

- Of course, be handsome

For several years after I was divorced, I did not date. Few responsible men are interested in marrying, or even dating, a woman who is a single mom with three young kids. Years pressed on and I crawled into bed exhausted and alone every night. Returning to college satisfied my desire for change and adventure for a while, and other projects and work kept me occupied.

As the children approached adolescence, I began to seriously wonder, "What does life hold for me?" My list hung on the back wall of my mind. Were there any men like the one on my list? None that I met.

I made the decision to jump back into the dating arena. Being a single parent for more than ten years made the leap awkward. Friends pushed and prodded. Soon I found myself in love with an ex-Navy man who was highly intelligent. I could check off, "Smarter than me." He had not left his wife, another check on the list. We attended church together, another check. However, a red flag went up when he exhibited moments of rash and embarrassing behaviors. One such incident occurred during a Sunday assembly of our singles' group. Our guest speaker was presenting a message when my Navy guy blurted, "Isn't that unfair to women?" so loudly that everyone froze. I sank, wishing the floor would swallow me, when I felt a friendly hand squeeze my shoulder from behind. It was a man named Sam. That was the beginning of a genuine friendship between Sam and me that developed slowly over four years into a romance after Navy guy and I split up.

I was on my way to NASA and looking forward to an exciting day. NASA was presenting a program for teachers of visually impaired students. I taught children who were blind and appreciated any guidance I could get. An overnight visit with my best friend, Sue, who lived near NASA, would be an added treat.

I would easily get to NASA in an hour on the familiar route that led to Houston. I was traveling at the speed limit of 55 mph as I came over an overpass. The cars in front of me were stopped cold! Someone was attempting to move a white trailer onto the freeway from the shoulder. Cars in both lanes slowed to a near stop. Which way should I go?

I slammed on the brakes. It was too late. My sedan hit the rear bumper of one of the cars. Air bags blew, I knew I had hit the car in front of me, but I didn't know what hit me. My face was numb. It must've hit the steering wheel. I ran my tongue over my teeth. They all seemed to be in place. Something felt terribly wrong. What had happened to my face?

"Ma'am," I heard a man in uniform say as he opened my car door, "Are you okay?"

He bent over, took one look, and moaned, "Oh, no!"

"We need an ambulance over here!" he screamed across the top of my car to others along the roadside.

Still so stunned I was afraid to imagine what I looked like. I was rigid in my seat and dared not look in the mirror.

Sympathetically he asked, "Is there someone I should call for you?"

My mind raced. Who should he call?

Sam and I had been dating each other for almost two years but with no commitments. Should I call my brother instead? Sam, a dentist, probably had an office full of patients. All his employees were preparing for a full day's work. He couldn't stop in the middle of a procedure.

Finally, I gave the officer Sam's work number, because I couldn't remember my brother's. What did I look like? How would he react?

"Ma'am, let me help you out," the officer said as he pried my foot off the brake pedal where it was still firmly pressed hoping to stop the disaster.

By this time, I realized I couldn't see with my left eye. Something wasn't right. "I need to go to an ophthalmologist." I kept repeating. No one responded. "Please just take me to an ophthalmologist." The ambulance took me directly to the hospital.

People scurried past me in the emergency room. Chills ran through my body. My legs began to tremble. "May I please have a blanket?" I spoke to thin air trying to get a nurse's attention. I trembled. Could they hear me? No one came.

But Sam came. My Hero. He was wearing his scrubs with "Dr. Sam" monogrammed over his left chest pocket which gave him more authority in this environment. A young nurse stuck a clipboard in my face and ordered, "Sign this." Sam pushed her clipboard aside. "Get her a blanket. She can sign that later."

Once under the blanket, the chills finally stopped and soon after a doctor looked at my eye. "You have a traumatic cataract." He seemed surprised. "You need to be taken to an ophthalmologist." Finally.

Sam carefully sat me in his car and drove me directly to the ophthalmologist. My face was still numb and my nose stung with a second-degree burn from the airbag. My face was swelling, raw, and bloody, but my heart was touched by Sam's tender care for me.

When the receptionists saw me at the eye clinic, they took me to the doctor immediately.

"You'll have an ugly eye," he said lacking any bedside manner. I still had not seen my face.

The airbag had slammed my glasses against my eye, destroying the pupil, ripping the iris, and permanently damaging the lens. The pupil would never close again.

In the following year, I had extensive surgery to the front part of my eye. Students from the Houston medical school were called in to observe this "unusual case." Before it was over, twenty doctors or soon-to-be doctors gawked at my "ugly eye." During the second surgery, damage to the macula was discovered. The macula is the spot on the retina where the most visual input takes place. This left me with a permanent slight blind spot in my left peripheral field.

Sam took care of me through it all, and he has ever since. As limited as my sight was that day, I could see clearly that Sam was a keeper. Trauma often reveals truth.

Sam met some requirements on my checklist but not all. He was equally handsome in a suit and jeans. He was a successful dentist and certainly smarter than me. He even sang in church, though he was more scientific than spiritual. However, he had been married twice. He had left his first wife. I began dating him a year after his second wife left and they were divorced.

I was determined and stubborn about plans for my future, and Sam knew I might not stay in the area much longer. I had no idea that Sam was making plans of his own, though I knew he was considering a new home. He had sold a large family house after his divorce and was living in a small rental house. One Sunday afternoon as we drove his old blue Suburban through a developing subdivision, he slowed down and said, "Which lot would you buy, this one or that one?"

"It should be your choice," I said. "It's for your house."

"What if it were your house? It could be." More than a little surprised, I chose the one I liked.

After four years of developing a true, loving friendship, Sam gave me a spectacular engagement ring. I took it to show my daughter who knew about diamonds. She examined it carefully counting the pavé diamonds under the solitaire. She said, "Mom, there are sixteen—one for every year you waited."

There is one thing about dating I'm sure of. And that is, *take your time.* Seems simple, doesn't it? It is not. So many rush love. Or they hurry marriage. Or they take the first one who shows any interest. Romantic love should stretch itself past the flowers and chocolates into action. In the long run, it is the kindness, the understanding, the forgiving, and the serving of one another that will sustain a true love relationship. A healthy relationship takes time to develop. Developing such relationships requires patience.

Sam and I went on to design and build our home. The hitch came as we planned our wedding. Our desire was to be married in the church where we had worshipped for several years.

In a meeting with our pastor to discuss our plans, he told us, "For me to marry you in this denomination you must sign this document." The document required us to state that any previous marriage ended for reasons approved in scripture.

Sam refused to sign it, and I don't sign documents regarding issues of the Spirit. My creator and I have an unwritten agreement. So, we were faced with a problem. If we were to marry, we would have to step around the rules of our own church. And we did.

Before you get the idea that I don't think rules are to be followed, I would like you to understand that rules are for the betterment of the people, but sometimes rules need to be examined. Not all rules should be followed blindly. Scripture is filled with men and women who stepped around the religious gatekeepers to do God's will. Here are a few examples from scripture.

The woman who touched Jesus' cloak broke Jewish law, because she was struggling with uncontrolled bleeding that the doctors of her day couldn't cure (Luke 8:44).

Rahab lied about hiding the Hebrew spies. God honored her due to her obedient faith in spite of her profession. It is believed she was a prostitute (Joshua 2: 2-4).

Tamar was a virtuous woman, who after being widowed twice was put aside by her father-in-law, Judah. Yet she risked everything, even her life, and certainly her reputation, to have a child. Children were the only source of support a woman had in those days, and to deny her the right to have children, was to deny her a future, as suggested in the Old Testament (Gen. 38: 15-16).

A dear pastor friend and his wife drove for six hours, and he performed the ceremony in a beautiful local church. One of my students, who happens to be blind, sang. Sam's daughter played the flute, and my two sons walked me down the aisle. All our children participated in our special day in some way. That was in 1996.

Over our years together, we have had a strong marriage, and through our union we have blessed many lives. What if I had insisted on following my checklist? What if we had not stepped around the rules? Because I ignored "the list" as well as someone else's unhealthy rules, our family has been blessed beyond measure.

- My daughter was able to travel to Russia where she found and adopted our granddaughter.

- My son survived a personal crisis.

- Another son received his first truck.

- My daughter had a "dad" that she so yearned for.

- I was free to resign a stressful job.

- I was free to speak at national conventions across the country.

- I was able to develop the SMORE for Women ministry.

- The SMORE ministry has blessed many single mothers.

- Sam and I are contributing members in our church, which, by the way, is not the same denomination that refused to bless our marriage.

Though I'm not an expert, these are simply a few things I've learned along the way—a long, long way. Before dating, do your homework. Learn about men. Not your dad or brother, but men who will have a different agenda in mind where you are concerned.

About men:

- Men are different from women. "Duh" you say, but how often do you expect a man to understand you—to be more like you?

- They think differently.

- They have different motivations.

- They have different agendas.

- Men have an agenda that involves satisfying their needs. And believe it or not, so do women.

- Men who truly love and are committed to you will go to great lengths to provide for and protect you.

- He will want to be in your presence.

- You will not have to call him. He will call you.

- He will recognize your value if you value yourself.

- You do teach the man how to treat you.

- Men need validation.

- Men need your respect.

- Men need to hear your compliments and acknowledgements.

Life is complicated and life as a Christian can be messy. There are many ideas in Christian circles about dating and relationships. Some are not even scriptural. I encourage single women to trust what the Bible has to say about relationships. Take the stars out of your eyes. Be fully aware that even one fling can change the course of your life. What I have today was certainly worth waiting for.

Seems simple, doesn't it? It is not. Above all, take your time. Good relationships don't just happen. They need time, patience and two people who truly want to be together.

SMORE TO CONSIDER

What are your feelings toward being single?

Mixed

Is there an area of your life that you have opened to unhealthy behaviors when it comes to dating? *boundaries self love*

[✓] Yes [ ] No

Are there areas in your life that you are willing to work on in order to attract a better-quality man? *Physical + mental fitness*

[✓] Yes [ ] No

What are some areas you think could use some improvement?

reading inner child. self worth picky inspire at age

When you are in a dating relationship how does your male friend respond when you say no to something he wants you to do?

Have you lived through at least one of life's crises or unpleasant situations while in the relationship? *2 deaths. / work issues.*

[✓] Yes [ ] No

How did that situation affect the relationship?

brought it closer.

References:
How to Not Date a Loser by Georgia Shaffer
The Automatic 2nd Date by Victorya Michaels Rogers
Finding a Man Worth Keeping by Victorya Michaels Rogers

CHAPTER EIGHT

Learning to Value Morality

Right is right even if no one is doing it; wrong is wrong even if everyone is doing it.

—Unknown

Where and when do ethics show up in our lives? I suggest that it is as early as infancy. A newborn learns early if his or her parents are trustworthy. The parent becomes the model. As Jeanie Miley, the author of *Joint Venture*, says, "When a child is born, the first question he begins asking, albeit unconsciously, is 'Who is in charge here?' and then, 'What do I have to do to get them to take care of me?'"[29] Part of taking care of children is teaching them how to navigate this world, and when they are young, they thrive on your love. They in reality need your love. As they grow into childhood, rules establish boundaries and, therefore, give them a sense of security.

Jesus taught us to be ethical, in other words to have a belief system or set of principles that govern our behavior and attitudes, and to apply our moral code, which defines our personal character, to that ethical system.

We've become a culture of experts at making excuses for our mistakes or what used to be called "sins." If I act wrongly, it must be because my parents mistreated me as a child. If I am not honest, my dishonest behavior is for my own best interest. If I harm a friend, well that's just how life goes sometimes, or maybe she even deserved it. The blame is deflected, and having a kind of integrity that owns the blame is not considered a virtue in today's corporate thinking.

We have also developed a culture with an attitude of entitlement. Too many seem to think the world owes them something. Even if I slip on a banana peel, it's someone else's fault. For example, an intoxicated Florida driver pled guilty to manslaughter then sued the estate of the victim he killed. In another case, parents sued the school after their son was kicked out of honors class for cheating. A maximum-security inmate who went to jail with five teeth sued the prison for dental problems. Our culture needs a return to an upright ethical system.

I realize there are times when the other party *is* at fault and some restitution is fair. For the most part, however, we have forgotten that life is not fair. Life is difficult and it always will be. None of us gets through it without challenges, and more often than anyone wants we experience real trials. Without ethics and morals, we have no guiding principles.

We attended our granddaughter Kaylin's baptism in Mobile, Alabama. It was an extra special occasion. In our faith's tradition, this important event follows a child's own personal decision to follow Christ. Of course, we attended the whole service, which just happened to be an interview between the pastor and a professor whose doctoral work was in eschatology, the scriptural study of end times. This is not a topic that interests me. In fact, I avoid it when at all possible. I was not in a position to escape this time, so I listened to their discussion of "pre" versus "post" millennialism, the rapture, and what is and is not negotiable. While I did not care for the topic, I appreciated the closing point most of all: we ought to consider that there is an end coming, so we should be ethical. Ethics is a topic that does interest me.

I gave Kaylin a plaque for her room as one of her baptismal gifts that day. It is a simply stated version of the Ten Commandments with all the bright colors for a young girl's room.

The Ten Commandments are more than just a good scene in a movie; they are simple rules to live by that work in any culture, nation, or neighborhood in the world. Please don't misunderstand me. I'm certainly not suggesting you return to the rigidity of the Old Testament, nor do I want to imply we create a simplistic religious environment, but I am suggesting that these ten rules were given to us for our benefit and if followed would make our world a much more pleasant place. We live near Cajun country, so the adaptation of the Ten Commandments that hangs on our kitchen wall goes like this:

God is number 1 . . . an daz all.
Don't pray to nuttin or nobody . . . jus' God.
Don't cuss nobody . . . 'specialy the Good Lord.
When it be Sunday . . . pass yo'self by God's House.
Yo mama and yo daddy dun did it all . . . lissen to dem.
Don't be kilt nobody.
God dun give you a wife . . . sleep wit' jus' her.
Don't go took nuthin' from nobody.
Always told dat whole troot.
Don't go wish fo yo' neighbors pirogue or tings.

As a parent, you are the one who must set the rules for your household. You can't be your child's buddy. At times this can be quite unpleasant, but it is part of the process of parenting. The Ten Commandments are a good, really good, starting point for setting the moral tone of your home.

I urge you to pay attention to these simple truths as you raise your children, teaching them to survive in this wild and crazy world. Let them know there are ethics, principles to live by, and that morals will put light on the path they walk. Choices and options may be simpler for them to figure out, and the results will bring with them a sense of purpose as well as personal and spiritual achievement.

Wise women:

- Demonstrate moral and ethical behaviors in their own life. Children do what they see.

- Talk about the importance values have in living a successful life.

- Emphasize developing the inner person as well as the outer person.

- Talk about character and how important it is to build a good one. I've heard it said that our children will do as we do, not what we tell them to do. Even if we think they are absorbed in their own world, and not paying attention to a thing we say—they are watching. It's the impression we leave that will make a difference to them and the choices they make. As a single mother, you may be the single biggest influence in your children's lives. Imagine you are walking along and stumble on a rock and fall into the mud; it's the impression you leave when you sink into the muck of life that your children will notice.

Friends and good manners will carry you where money won't go.[30]

—Margaret Walker

You may wonder why I would bring up manners in a chapter on ethics and morals, but the fact is, morality isn't only about not doing bad behaviors, it's also about doing the right behaviors. Learning manners is one of our first steps on the path of morality. We need to teach children good manners, the earlier the better. Learning what to say and when to say it is the basis of most manners.

Simple manners children should learn first include the following: (Check out the resource links on the SMORE To Consider page.)

- Say "Please" when asking for something.
- Say "Thank You" when receiving something.
- Say "Excuse me" if you must interrupt others who are talking.
- Say "Thank you" after eating your meal.
- Say "Hello" when someone says hello to you.
- Look at a person's face when talking to them.

Children are not the only people who need to learn manners; adults need manners as well. It is easy to be polite when everything is running smoothly, but such is not the case when you've been hurt or even abused. To remain civil in the presence of someone who has hurt you is harder than you'd think, especially with an ex-spouse. If possible, remind yourself who this person is to your children. If so, never get into a heated argument in their presence. They are already feeling uneasy knowing the two of you are at odds. You are the model for your children, and they will remember if you cause a scene where they are caught in the middle, no matter how justified you are. In some cases, as with other relatives, the conversation can be postponed. If you feel you are about to say something you will regret, excuse yourself, leave the room, and regain your composure.

If you do lose your temper in front of your children, apologize quickly with a simple explanation, steering clear of blame or shame. It is difficult for most women I know not to overreact to words intended to jab or criticize. When you are facing an encounter, (and you know one will come) be prepared and mind your manners.

It's not just what we say that counts, but what we write in our emails, tweets, and Facebook posts that can cause a bit of trouble. In today's world we are faced with a new dilemma: digital manners. We have new choices to make, such as when, or if, to answer a cell call when visiting with friends. I feel a few courtesies apply here:

- Put people first in all situations.
- Excuse yourself to accept important calls.
- Never talk loudly in public places.
- Do not share messages or photos without permission.
- Be considerate.
- Never, ever text while driving.

As a parent, it is imperative to be alert to what your child is doing online. The same simple manners listed previously should apply to children's behavior online. Now more than ever, it's important to teach our children boundaries, especially on the internet. A child, even a teenager, isn't capable of understanding how their actions online can affect their future. They simply haven't lived long enough. Parents must have strict rules about online behavior. It is a matter of safety as well as basic manners. Ultimately, you are modeling respect for others. Respect is the core of good manners.

One Christmas season I was walking through Walmart when I saw a totally distracted mom texting on her phone. Struggling a few steps in front of her was her young son trying to push the cart, gripping the handle that he could barely reach. He looked up at me apologetically. It's too easy to take into adulthood the poor habits that are practiced during the teen years. An important rule to follow is this: do not be distracted by technology. Instead, pay attention to what is happening around you; someone's welfare or life may depend on it.

Teaching kids to behave requires consistency. Consistency is of the utmost importance when raising kids. When a child is disciplined one time and ignored for the same behavior another time, they become confused about what is right and wrong. When they can't figure out what to expect from a parent or when the parent reacts in opposite ways, indifference results. The child comes to feel that it doesn't matter what he or she does one way or the other, and in worst-case scenarios, he or she loses all sense of what is right or wrong as well as empathy for others. Tragic individuals without conscience come from such circumstances.

While teaching high school, I noticed a wide range of differences in the behaviors of students. Most could be attributed to the apple not falling far from the tree. Parents, who curse at their kids and allow teenagers to curse them back, have missed the boat on manners. Parents, who defend their child's behavior or even suggest the teacher is to blame when told of his or her misconduct, miss the ship. Parents who encourage their kids to disrespect authority miss their flight. Raising a child in a too vulgar or coddled environment can surely set your kid up for a lifetime of failure.

"Three things in human life are important: the first is to be kind; the second is to be kind; and the third is to be kind."[31]

—Henry James

Kindness is one of the tenets of good manners. It is a starting point on which others are built. How do you teach your children to live in harmony with other human critters? How can you train them to be nice?

Prior to age four children should be taught simple manners: To say, "Excuse me," "Please," and "I'm sorry." Around age four or five children, who have been taught to have empathy for others, begin to demonstrate a more personal and sometimes genuine compassion for others. To get there, however, parents must demonstrate empathy and kindness for children to catch on.

I recall my first experience with empathy. My cousin Kay had taken me to a movie. In the movie, a circus parade was coming into town and Emmett Kelly, the famous clown, was riding on one of the cars. He was playing and showing off with a deck of cards when he lost control and flipped all the cards onto the street below. He began to cry as only Emmett Kelly could do with his sad clown face—and so did I. All the onlookers watching the parade laughed. Everyone in the movie theater was laughing. Not me. I was so upset Kay had to take me home sobbing, and we missed the remainder of the movie. I didn't get the humor, but I certainly had empathy, probably, at least in part, because my mother had taught me to think about how the other person felt, and to be kind.

Situations in which it is most difficult to be kind may be the ones when kindness is needed the most. I like what the Dalai Lama said: "Be kind whenever possible. It is always possible."

Life is harsh with many sharp edges. Most of our injuries come from other humans just like us. "Hurt people, hurt people" as they say in Alcoholics Anonymous. We can stop this cycle with kindness.

Why do we have "How to" books and articles about every human condition imaginable? You can Google any situation to find instant solutions or advice from so called self-appointed experts, and yet so many of our problems could be solved with kindness. As a single parent, you are in the position to raise kind children. We must teach our children that Christ's powerful, yet simple message is still viable today: Love one another. Be kind.

When Christ was asked, "Which is the greatest commandment?" He gave us what could be considered an eleventh commandment:

"Let me give you a new commandment. Love one another. In the same way I loved you, you love one another. This is how everyone will recognize that you are my disciples—when they see the love you have for each other" (John 13:34, MSG).

There can be no confusion about what he meant. We can be confused and uncertain about pre- and postmillennialism, but not about this—I suggest that more attention be given to the simple, though rare, tenet of the Christian faith: love one another.

Gratitude is powerful. Recent research suggests that children who express gratitude are better adjusted and do better in school than those who do not. Diana Kapp, in *The Wall Street Journal*, reported that:

Among a group of 122 elementary school kids taught a weeklong curriculum on concepts around giving, gratitude grew, according to a study published in 2014 in *School Psychology Review*. The heightened thankfulness translated into action: 44% of the kids in the curriculum opted to write thank-you notes when given the choice following a PTA presentation. In the control group, 25% wrote notes. According to Kapp, *Gratitude works like a muscle. Take time to recognize good fortune, and feelings of appreciation can increase.*[32]

You may contribute to a happy family by implementing times for expressing gratitude in your routines. It worked for me. The first summer I moved my three young children to Austin where I attended the University of Texas; we lived in a small two-bedroom apartment. The children had no choice in the matter and were anything but happy the first few days. I realized I must do something to shift the attitude, or we were in for a long, hot summer. Each night at bedtime I asked them to tell three things they were thankful for. It became the "three thank-you's" and it turned their moods around. I have found that yelling at a child to be grateful doesn't do the trick. One of the few things my dad said about raising children was, "Save your 'No' for those times and situations that involve moral issues, so the child will be more inclined to listen." They may appear not to listen, but they do hear every word you say.

SMORE TO CONSIDER

If you were to give yourself a score for moral behavior, where would you fall on this line?

Not so good   Pretty proud of myself
1 --- 2 --- 3 --- 4 --- 5 --- 6 --- 7 --- 8 --- 9 --- 10

What score would you give each of your children as to manners?

Not so good   I'm proud of my kiddos
1 --- 2 --- 3 --- 4 --- 5 --- 6 --- 7 --- 8 --- 9 --- 10

How do your children act in public?

What area(s) would you like to work on with your kids?

What recent act of kindness have you done and for whom?

How did that make you feel?

CHAPTER NINE

Loving the Fun

A cheerful heart does good like medicine, but a broken spirit makes one sick.
—Proverbs 17:22 (LTB)

Having fun comes more easily for some than others. If you are a natural fun-loving mom, you could probably write this chapter. If, however, you need a few pointers, I hope you will apply these to achieve more fun and laughter in your home.

I have never been good with fun for fun's sake. If fun can be incorporated into another activity, I am all for it. I was raised in a no-nonsense home, so planning to have fun was just not done. I enjoyed time with my cousins and neighborhood friends, but usually my idea of fun was a little more industrious, like making doll clothes. Play, in my day, required imagination. So, when I had three little ones of my own, I organized groups for them such as The Traveling Treehouse Troopers. My friends and I arranged for our preschoolers to have outings that were fun and enriching. They all had matching T-shirts, and the moms cooperated in taking them to area spots of interest such as the fire station. Although it's popular today, I didn't play with my children; I thought that was what children did with each other.

One thing I did was to schedule time with each child. When my children were young, I would place a note on the calendar for a "Special Day" for each child. On that date, I took that child alone for a day or most of a day, and we did things they enjoyed. Our day never involved shopping or going to buy a toy. We shared a variety of activities. One day I took my son to the sea wall on the Intracoastal Waterway in Port Arthur, Texas, and we walked along and talked about why it was there. Other times we might go to a park. Whatever we did it always involved one-on-one conversation. My children are now in their forties, and I can tell you even those few simple "Special Days" made a difference. If you make the effort, even ordinary situations can become family fun memories.

If you must hold yourself up to your children as an object lesson, hold yourself up as a warning and not as an example.[33]

—George Bernard Shaw

A road trip is an excellent way to create fun family memories. Of course, it will take planning and saving. Remember that for children almost every experience is new. You may have been on the same road trip many times, but for them it could be the trip of a lifetime. It doesn't have to be a big adventure. It might be a picnic on the way to a beach, a trip to the amusement park, or a visit to grandmother's house. One trip we took required planning and saving. But our greatest memory was unplanned.

Somehow, I had managed to save enough money for us to go to the family friendly Sipapu Ski Resort, in New Mexico, for a winter vacation. My nephew Cliff, who is only ten years my junior, was free to travel with us. It was wonderful to have a man along to help with the driving as well as for safety and support; besides, the kids loved him, and he is a great photographer. So, after packing three kids, my nephew, and me into our station wagon, we headed out across Texas—850 miles, with maroon luggage bags strapped on the rack, loads of enthusiasm, and dreams of a skiing adventure in our heads.

After the long trip, we arrived at the small resort nestled in the side of a mountain. Snow covered everything and the buildings reminded me of a European village. Our quarters, overlooking the stream that separated the facilities from the ski slopes, were lovely.

The children took ski lessons from a Native American who adored them. He taught them how to snow plow with their skis so they could control their speed. They used a Poma lift, which is a small T-bar that you straddle and it pulls you up the hill. The rules were clear—do not point your skis straight down the hill. No "flying" is allowed down the baby slope, which is reserved for children nine and younger. This rule was lost on Damon who thoroughly enjoyed the speed and thrill. He was told he would have his lift pass pulled if he kept it up. Lance, my youngest, who was barely six, spent most of the day crawling up and sliding down. Skiers had to be at least nine years old to ride the chair lift up the adult ski slopes. Treva, just nine, continued to beg me to take her up. I finally gave in.

"When we get to the first terminal, you need to stand up," I told her. "The chair will keep moving upward. So be ready. The chair will slow only slightly." She did just as I said, but I froze. She landed in the snow next to the stand.

"Mom!" Treva screamed at me as she lay looking up from the snow. The chair continued moving with me in it. The lift operator rushed out and looked up at me as I was being pulled higher up the hill.

"Lady, can you ski down from the top?"

"No!" I hollered down.

"We'll call the ski patrol."

"Take care of my daughter," I begged.

"We will. She will be fine," he assured me.

I rode higher and higher. I was a novice skier. What in the world would I do? At the top of the mountain, I found a map on a post. All the paths down were Black Diamond, not easy slopes. I went a few steps. Two young men saw my hesitation.

"Ma'am, do you need some help?"

"Yes, which way should I go?"

"You can ski down this way, or go around the ledge to your left." They were off in a flash. I approached the ledge since the snow path in front of me was a 45-degree slope straight down. I soon realized the ledge was narrow and steep. Frustrated and frightened, I sat in the snow up to my waist. I thought of Robert Frost, who wrote in the poem, "The Road Not Taken:"

> I shall be telling this with a sigh
> Somewhere ages and ages hence:
> Two roads diverged in a wood, and I,
> I took the one less traveled by,
> And that has made all the difference.[34]

I had no idea what I should do. Should I try to ski down one of these slopes? Minutes seemed like hours.

"Here she is," a man called out. Two ski patrol officers smiled at me.

"Do you want to be carried down in a basket?"

"No," I was embarrassed.

"Come over here," one of them instructed me to position myself to the extreme side of the slope. I did as he said while the other one went to the opposite side a little bit farther down.

"Now," my instructor said, "Go to him and don't look down. Just look at him," pointing to the other patrol officer. So, it went. I crossed the slope at sharp angles all the way down the mountain.

My kids weren't spared embarrassment. They told me how others were asking, "Did you hear about the lady who went to the top and had to be helped down?"

Plan an adventure with your children. It could be a real memory maker. It might be messy. Everything might not turn out just right. That's okay too. Allow your children to see how you react in these situations. Your example will teach them a great deal about how to handle life's little surprises.

You can make fun out of everyday life. After my divorce, I was hired by a school district that was forty minutes north of our home; I knew I needed a car that got better gas mileage than the one I had. I found a kelly-green Toyota station wagon, and I thought I was lucky when I bought it for $3000 from the previous owner, who was an ex-Marine. It was a standard stick shift, and I hadn't driven a standard in years. After piling all three children into it and heading down the road, I quickly realized this would take some practice. As we lurched along, one of the kids said, "Mom, why are we jumping? It's like Kermit the Frog."

So, our "new" car was dubbed "Kermit." I hung a tiny Kermit the Frog, from the rearview mirror. We traveled many miles in Kermit, and to this day, the Kermit that hung from the windshield has a special place in my kitchen china cabinet. It still brings a smile to my grown children's faces.

For several years at the beginning of December, we went with a church group to Dickens on the Strand in Galveston, Texas. It is Galveston's world-famous Victorian holiday festival. The children had the experience of seeing that adults can have clean fun together without a spouse. We all dressed up in Victorian era costumes and had a ball seeing the sights, singing carols, and enjoying the start of the Christmas season to come.

The creation of something new is not accomplished by the intellect, but by the play instinct.[35]

—Carl Jung

"Boys need to be building things, working with tools," I said to my friend Stephanie. I had a daughter, eight years old, and two sons, seven and five. She had two sons in the same age range.

"Ha," Stephanie laughed. "And what can we do about that?" she challenged with that mischievous British expression she had when an idea was brewing. Stephanie had come out of a seriously abusive marriage, and yet she met the challenge courageously.

Her powerful choleric personality (natural-born leader), though suppressed in her marriage, was in full bloom as a single mother with a job as a home health care nurse.

"Didn't you say you needed a doghouse for the puppy?" she asked.

"Yes," I replied, "the kids hate to leave her outside, and I don't want her in the house."

"Well, we could help them build a dog house."

"Stephanie!" I retaliated. Her ideas often seemed too out of range for my practical way of thinking. "How can we do that? We would need saws and lumber. We can't manage all that." I was the undisciplined and unorganized playful sanguine.

"They sell keets for people like uz." Her British accent was coming through.

"They, who?" I wanted to know.

Well, Stephanie persisted as any good powerful choleric would, and we did find a doghouse building kit at a local home improvement store. It included precut pieces, nails, and roofing shingles. We set a date for construction.

I insisted the workday must be fun. Stephanie, in her take charge way, had a plan. That day we made memories as well as a doghouse. It was a great success, and the doghouse was painted, repainted, and re-roofed numerous times over the years. It became a symbol and memento of a day none of us would forget. My inspiring and playful memories changed only slightly after reviewing the day with my then thirty-something children. Damon, my eldest son, pointed out that there are some things single moms should consider carefully as they plan such a project.

- Don't use a tack hammer for roofing nails.

- Don't give more than one kid a paintbrush.

- Lay down plastic if painting is to be done over the grass.

- Finally, consider the weight of the finished project. (We had to find someone who could lift and haul it back to our house.)

New research coming out indicates that sharing a family meal has lasting value. Your dinner table can be a time for family togetherness and a bit of teamwork: food preparation, setting and clearing the table, telling funny stories, and a place for sharing the events of the day. The time spent with family at the dinner table builds bonds and helps children learn better communication skills. Dinnertime becomes a time for parents and children to establish ties that last. It can even be a time and place where traditions are born. Most of us who grew up having family meals can recall a few special moments. Surely, one or two were fun.

The Family Dinner Project https://thefamilydinnerproject.org is a website that offers wonderful examples and tips to make your family dinner table a special place. If sitting down at a family table is not something you are used to doing, here are a few table topic ideas:

- Tell the best moment of your day.

- Leave an empty chair and have each person imagine who he or she would like to have sitting there and why. Share questions you would like to ask the person.

- Say something nice about the person to your right.

- Tell what you would do if you won the lottery.

- Tell something nice you would like to do for someone you love.

You may be amazed at the shift in attitudes with your children. At first, they may not like eating away from the television, but they will get used to it and even look forward to it.

Creating family meal memories may be overwhelming to think about, especially when you are wondering how you will get all the laundry done, put a meal on the table, and pay the bills. But, trying to have at least one family meal a week will be worth it, even if it takes a bit of planning or budgeting for something really special.

If you are the orderly sort of person or like planning details, meal planning may come naturally to you. But, if you are the fly-by-the-seat-of-your-pants type person, your focus may be more on fun than orderliness. You may want to partner with a friend who likes to make a project happen and who will help keep you on track—the more the merrier, anyway.

The kitchen is a great place to create positive attitudes about cooking and eating healthy foods. As the mother, you can introduce both your daughters and sons to the art of cooking. Gender roles have loosened up; more men are entering the cooking arts while more women are drawn to the sciences than in the past. Every child needs to learn how to function in the kitchen.

The best thing about creating great childhood memories for your kids is that memories can be made anywhere; they don't need to be gigantic vacations. They can be plain old run-of-the-mill activities.

Here are a few ideas:

- Plan a menu and prepare a meal for friends. Have the kids make invitations and place cards.

- Plan and prepare for a party.

- Plant a flower or vegetable garden, or just pot a plant in a container.

- Gift wrap a present.

- Build a birdhouse or bird feeder with a kit.

- Find a book in the library and check it out.

- Bake a cake and decorate it. Take it to a friend, teacher, or grandparent.

- Wash and wax the car.

- Remember something you learned from a parent and share it with your children.
- Paint a piece of furniture.
- Have a Name Your Car campaign.
- Let the kids make a favorite dessert.
- Help the kids make a birthday card for a grandparent.
- Take silly photos of each other and display on your refrigerator.
- Put small jigsaw puzzles together.
- Leave an ongoing Scrabble game out.
- Let children paint a pillowcase with fabric paints.
- Rake leaves into a pile and jump in.
- Go to a bookstore and let the child buy an inexpensive book to read aloud to you.
- Let the child style your hair.
- Paint everyone's toenails.
- Make chalk designs on the driveway then wash it off.
- Test how many different ways you can flavor popcorn.
- Make peanut butter pinecone bird feeders.
- Make a family video and post on Facebook.
- Have younger children wrap up in sheets and act out a story.
- Have a tea party.
- Go to a park, bring sandwiches, and play Frisbee.
- Visit a local museum.
- Cut craft foam into shapes, and use as bathtub toys that stick to tiles when wet.
- Go hiking in a wooded trail.
- Roast marshmallows and make s'mores.

Whatever you do, give your child the freedom to express his or her true personality in the process. Remember, children don't do everything perfectly and that is okay. Let them have fun with the process.

Church activities also offer wholesome ways to have fun. Church attendance has the advantage of helping you make acquaintances with people who share your values. Some of my kids' summer camp friendships built strong bonds, they were in one another's weddings and still stay in touch even though they no longer live nearby.

Some of my fondest memories are of my children laughing with their friends. The laughter of a child is like a healing balm for the hurts you have experienced. Create an atmosphere for laughter in your home.

SMORE TO CONSIDER

What is a fun memory from your childhood?

Many times, we don't plan "adventures" with our children, because we think we can't afford it, but many wonderful times can be had for free. Think of several things in or near your town that are free—parades, museums, walking trails, beaches, etc.

1.
2.
3.
4.
5.

Which of these activities would you like to do first?

Do you let your children cook with you?

[ ] Yes[ ] No

Why, or why not?

Do you see mealtime as "family time?"

[ ] Yes[ ] No

What would have to change in your routine in order to have a sit-down family meal?

CHAPTER TEN

Loving the Growth

God never put anyone in a place too small to grow .

—Henrietta Mears

Spring is one of God's great examples of anticipation, rivaled only by pregnancy. The air is filled with expectancy and little bits of green sprout through the brown surface of pressed grass. Trees bud with tender baby leaves. As Alexander Pope suggested, "Hope springs eternal."[36]

Growth of all things amazes me. I enjoy looking at sprouting trees, budding flowers, and of course, children as they grow and change almost daily. Isn't that what it's all about—growth? Our physical growth is not of our own doing, but our spiritual growth is another matter: We must be willing for that growth to happen. For me—that is what life is all about yet we resist the very situations that cause, or force us to grow. Sometimes this kind of growth is more than uncomfortable—it's painful. That is why we call them growing pains.

Through each of the experiences I have shared, I grew. I learned. I can't say any of the experiences were pleasant, but I can say they made me a better person. Struggles came and like most, I resisted. My resistance only made each experience harder to endure. My stubborn nature didn't help.

Life forced spiritual growth in my life garden. I'm still growing. First, like it or not, this is a lifelong journey. Hebrews 6:1 (MSG) says, " . . . Let us continue progressing towards maturity." No one is born spiritually mature. It is a process. Secondly, it is not something that automatically happens as we age. Bible study and church attendance are good things, but in and of themselves they do not bring spiritual maturity. Experiences in our life plant the seeds, but we need to do the

watering, pruning (cleaning up dead stuff in our lives), and protecting of
the new growth from hazardous elements. Becoming a spiritual gardener
is not easy; we must be willing to accept God's way for us.

I once had a friend who said with sarcasm every time something
difficult happened, "Oh, dear, here comes another opportunity for
spiritual growth." As I look back, I think I can say without a doubt, it is
these circumstances, the ones that cause us the greatest pain, that bring us
the greatest gain in our spiritual journey. Growth that produces strength
often comes through resistance. The circumstances we face may bring out
or develop a strength we didn't know we had or didn't know was possible.

James 1:2-4 says, "When troubles come your way, consider it
an opportunity for great joy. For you know that when your faith is
tested, your endurance has a chance to grow. So let it grow, for when
your endurance is fully developed, you will be perfect and complete,
needing nothing" (NLT).

Growth is for the most part uncomfortable. Physically, it takes
energy. Mentally, it requires effort. Spiritually, it comes as a surprise like a
guest at your back door that you weren't prepared for.

For those of us who grew up in church, there is a phenomenon
that can and often does happen: we become SMUGIR: Spiritually
Minded Unless Growth Is Required. We attend church. We are even
active in church. We think we have all the answers. We feel comfortable
knowing we are right, not righteous, but right. We would rather dig out
a scripture reference than admit that the quandaries we face are mysteries,
and only God knows the answer. We become SMUGIR.

Spiritual growth doesn't happen simply at our request. It isn't
reading scriptures or devotions daily. It isn't saying prayers every morning.
It isn't attending church every Sunday.

Spiritual growth brings us to our knees. It puts us in our place.
Surrender is necessary, and we don't surrender very well. Ask us to
organize a committee? We can do that. Ask us to plan a new wing for
the church? We like that. Ask us to raise funds for the underprivileged?
That would be an honor and bring us praise. We like that. Ask us to be in
charge of a meal for the grieving, and we know just what to do. But ask
us to dig in deep and listen for direction from our holiest friend and we
resist. We do not know how.

When transformation occurs, it comes through God's will and
our willingness. We must not be smug. SMUGIR isn't a place you want
to stay for long, not if you want to grow. Smug refers to pride, spiritual

pride, and can be very dangerous for those around you as well as for yourself. When others go through trials, we rationalize in our spiritual pompousness, "If she would just do such and such, then she wouldn't be in this fix." We must be on guard against these thoughts because someday that person could be us. Though it is true, some actions obviously lead to heartbreak while others lead to safety, we need to plant compassion in our spiritual gardens as part of our growth.

Another lesson I've learned about spiritual growth is that other people are often the sandpaper used to smooth out our rough edges. In order to grow we need to be in relationships with people, even people we don't like. In these situations, we learn about ourselves:

- How we react.
- How we feel towards them.
- How, or if, we are capable of showing compassion.
- How willing we are to forgive injustices.
- What our personal weaknesses are.
- How unlike Christ we really are.

Sometimes when we experience trouble and wrestle like Jacob did with the angel, we find ourselves out of joint. It is the only time most of us truly discover that we must let go, that we can't change the world, and that we are not in control of others. Then the greatest power steps up, we hand over the controls, and grace, amazing grace teaches us about growth.

One of my favorite authors, , wrote a small book published in 1975 titled *Adventures in Prayer*. In chapter 5 of "The Prayer of Relinquishment," she states, ". . . the giving up of self-will is the hardest thing we human beings are ever called on to do." She addresses our fears when she says, "As we force ourselves to walk up to the fear and look it full in the face—never forgetting that God and His power are still the supreme reality—the fear evaporates." Finally, she says, "I saw that a demanding spirit, with self-will as its rudder, blocks prayer."[37]

As Catherine Marshall so eloquently reminds us, peace will creep into our heart when we understand the power of God, so let go and let God.

So often, we refer to our lives as being on a journey. I refer to it as "my path." I think each path is uniquely designed for us to travel, a path where we will learn and grow. Your path may seem too rough, crooked, or twisty, and you feel that other people's lives are so much easier than yours. If our focus is on what others have, we can miss the beauty, rich lessons, and values of our journey. Acceptance of the path you walk brings much more peace than does constantly comparing your life to that of others.

As a mom you hold the hands of your little ones walking beside you. You warn them of the obstacles. You point out ways to choose the wise routes, take the best turns, and avoid danger. If your child stumbles, you help him up, brush him off, kiss any bruises, and continue. Whatever missteps they make, you love them still. One day you release them to blaze their own trail. Aren't most of us just like that, trying to make our way?

I'm telling you, once and for all, that unless you return to square one and start over like children, you're not even going to get a look at the kingdom, let alone get in (Matthew 18: 3 MSG).

Keep in mind, you are not alone on this path; the gospel of Matthew leaves us with this promise. ". . . And I will be with you always, to the end of the age" (Matt 28:20 NIV). Whatever steps or missteps you take—remember they are mostly baby steps and Jesus the Christ loves you.

As the founder of SMORE for Women, I hear heartbreaking stories from single mothers who are making every effort to hold their homes together. As the head of a household and with limited earning power, they continue to move forward and hold their heads high. The reasons for being a single mom are diverse: divorce, death of a spouse, or becoming pregnant in an uncommitted relationship.

Many had unhappy childhoods with no responsible parent setting an example. Even simple decisions can become overwhelming, paralyzing them. Those who do have a family support system still suffer the emotional disappointments of shattered dreams. During our Day of Blessings, we pamper our moms with a spa day, as well as offering workshops and coaching; we try to put together as many resources as we can to encourage our single moms. When we feel we have the tools to do the job, there is hope, and where there is hope, there is courage to face another day.

There is power in acceptance. Acceptance is facing the reality of an undesirable situation. Acceptance doesn't mean we ignore our feelings; it means we acknowledge them, address them, and advance onward. I have a different kind of AAA for safety on this journey of single mothering: Accept, Acknowledge, and Advance. Acceptance is key. Peter McWilliams explains it well:

Acceptance is not a state of passivity or inaction. I am not saying you can't change the world, right wrongs, or replace evil with good. Acceptance is, in fact, the first step to successful action. If you don't fully accept a situation precisely the way it is, you will have difficulty changing it. Moreover, if you don't fully accept the situation, you will never really know if the situation should be changed.[38]

The idea of acceptance may make you feel like you are throwing in the towel, but it's not really like that. It's just being honest—seeing things for what they really are, good or bad. Here is where truth can play a part in making future decisions. What are your choices? You can fight it. You can try to fix it, or you can flow with it.

No matter how badly we think life has beaten us, we still cling to the idea that acceptance and surrender are a kind of hopeless giving in, a weakness of character. Not so! Acceptance means simply admitting there are things we cannot change. Accepting them puts an end to our futile struggles and frees our thought and energy to work on things that can be changed. Surrender means relinquishing our self-will and accepting God's will and His help.[39]

—*One Day at a Time in Al-Anon*

You can let the actions of others trip you up. You can react with anguish, hurt, and anger. You can spend a great deal of energy blaming others for your circumstances, but as long as you are focused on blaming another, even if it's justified, you are giving away your power. Even blaming yourself for your situation is a huge energy drain. Acceptance of *what is* brings peace, so you can move on.

Somewhere along our path we learned to be self-critical. You may not be as kind to yourself as you are to others. Why can I give grace to someone else and not myself? Here's where the power of acceptance comes in; when we accept ourselves just as we are, we then have the power to change what needs to change and unconditionally love ourselves on the journey, no matter what. The next time you hear the old messages playing in your head; hit the pause button and then delete. I learned that criticism and condemnation of others is a waste of my precious energy. When I let myself go to that poisoned well, it takes me away from the place I need to be.

When we are real with ourselves, we will find freedom, freedom from guilt, shame, perfectionism, blame, and a critical spirit. Denial will hold us hostage for as long as we let it. It is our choice to open the door to a better future, by accepting the things that are, right now.

In 1922, Helen Howarth Lemmel wrote one of my favorite hymns, "Turn Your Eyes Upon Jesus." She was born in England, immigrated to the United States as a child with her family, studied music in Germany, and married a wealthy European. Even though she was a world-renowned Christian singer and songwriter, her husband abandoned her when she lost her eyesight. He left her to struggle with multiple heartaches during her midlife years. In 1918, at age 55, Helen was handed a tract by a missionary friend that was titled "Focused." In it was the statement, "So then, turn your eyes upon Him, look full into His face and you will find that the things of earth will acquire a strange new dimness." After hearing the statement, she is quoted saying, "I stood still, and singing in my soul and spirit was the chorus, with not one conscious moment of putting word to word to make rhyme, or note to note to make melody. The verses were written the same week, after the usual manner of composition, but nonetheless dictated by the Holy Spirit."[40]

I liked this song long before my first husband left me and before I taught children who were blind. It just has more meaning now that I know the story behind it. When raising children as a single mom, you will need to walk closely with the Spirit. I know no other way than to pull tightly into Him for strength when my path gets scary. Helen's words say it best.

O soul, are you weary and troubled?
No light in the darkness you see?
There's light for a look at the Savior, and life more
abundant and free!
Turn your eyes upon Jesus,
Look full in His wonderful face,
And the things of earth will grow strangely dim,
In the light of His glory and grace.[41]

—Helen Howarth Lemmel, Turn Your Eyes Upon Jesus

SMORE TO CONSIDER

What truth(s) has your path or journey shown you?

    1.
    2.
    3.
    4.
    5.

Where do you feel the most growth is taking place in your life right now?

Who do you consider your "sandpaper?"

Why do you think this?

What thing(s) are you struggling to accept?

Can you believe God will take care of your needs?

Stop for a minute and meditate on the face of Jesus. What do you see?

CHAPTER ELEVEN

Loving the Power of Prayer

Prayer is not getting things from God. Prayer is getting into perfect communion with God.

—Oswald Chambers, *Prayer*

Prayer can be a scream, a cry, or a whisper.
Prayer is forgiving our self and others.
Prayer is pleading with Almighty God.
Prayer is a yearning to have our way.
Prayer is a conversation.
Prayer is being grateful.
Prayer is being sorry.

I think prayer is highly misunderstood. I believe this is the case even in our churches. We say memorized words of prayers ritualistically. We shout prayers or say them silently. Usually, we are begging the creator of the universe to change something or do something our way. Isn't this preposterous, that we should tell the greatest power, the omnipotent, and all knowing what we think should be done? Harry Emerson Fosdick said it best, "Of all misconceptions of prayer, none is more common than the idea that it is a way of getting God to do our will."[42]

Instead of using prayer to get what you want, I truly believe that we were meant to stay in an attitude of prayer all the time. We are to keep the connection open so to speak. We are to continue to trust God in all things. Our faith is to remain strong, and this is prayer at its best.

As a young mother I seldom, if ever, prayed. I married a man who had no use for church but claimed it was okay for me to go. He certainly didn't pray. He was self-dependent, not God-reliant. I was in a godless marriage. God had not left me. I had turned away. I did not pray, not really, for years. I attended church off and on, always alone.

My first child was four months old, and we had recently moved back to my hometown so that my husband could join my brother's family business. When we had just been there a few weeks, my dad was rushed to the Houston Diagnostic Hospital, seriously ill. I would get a daily report by phone. One day I stood next to the yellow wall phone and talked with my mother about Daddy's condition. After that call, I prayed. For the first time in years I asked, "God, whatever is best for everyone." The next day Daddy died.

The Spirit pricked my soul, and I promised the Lord from that day forward I would pray and not ever quit. I might not understand it. I certainly can't comprehend the power of prayer. Even though it often makes no sense to me—I pray.

As a single mother of three, for five years I managed to control the dilemmas we faced. I was determined to overcome each obstacle without depending on others. This unexpected hiccup, whatever it was, would be just another in our day-in, day-out struggle—or so I thought.

When my nine-year-old son, Damon, complained, "My stomach hurts," I thought he had a virus. Hours later, he was curled up in a tight ball unaware of his older sister, Treva, and younger brother, Lance, playing nearby. I knew this was not a virus.

My knees buckled with fear, as I scooped up his drooping body, and carried him to the car. His thin limbs spread out on the car seat like a worn-out stuffed toy. I prodded and hustled the other children into the backseat and sped to the doctor's office. Dr. Forsythe rushed in and examined Damon quickly. He spoke with clipped and quick phrases.

"I think his appendix has ruptured. We must get him to the hospital right away," he spoke without looking up from the report he was writing.

Surely, they can fix it, I thought. I can handle this—my take-charge manner kicked in.

"We don't have time to wait for an ambulance. You'll drive him to the hospital," the grave tone in his voice was alarming. "The surgeon is waiting for you in the emergency room."

My thoughts were switched to auto replay. Appendix ruptured. Surgeon waiting. I'd heard of appendicitis. People get it all the time. I wasn't as sure about the "ruptured" part. I gripped the wheel, flipped on the emergency flashers and drove, as fast as reasonably safe.

The surgeon and staff were waiting. Dr. Adams touched Damon's tight and swollen tummy gently. His eyes met mine. He frowned. Even this seasoned surgeon seemed surprised as he said, "His appendix has ruptured." He ordered the staff, "Set up for surgery stat." My heart seemed to stall; a trembling started from my gut that worked its way to my fingertips. I had no choices. My child's life was totally out of my control. I called Damon's dad at work.

The anesthesiologist came clip-clopping down the hall in his wooden shoes. He was Dutch, and his wooden shoes added to the unreal feel of the situation. Was I watching a television drama? This couldn't be as bad as it appeared to be. I was always the one in charge. What could happen?

They prepped Damon for surgery. I stood by helpless, watching the medical staff performing specific tasks with deliberate actions. Damon grew sleepy from the sedatives. I ached to hold him as I had when he was a colicky baby, but he lay helpless, nearly unconscious. The white linens, white straps across his legs, and white uniforms created a pure image of light, but darkness filled my heart with denial. This couldn't be happening. He was jumping, laughing, and playing yesterday. I walked beside the stretcher rolling its way to the operating room. In the sterile corridor outside the entrance doors to surgery, Damon lay on the stretcher under crisp sheets tightly in place with his little arms folded across his chest almost as pale as the linens that held him. He looked like a corpse. "Say 'Goodbye' to your son," the nurse said.

A resistance yelled from the depth of my being.

"No!"

The echo came back, "Noooooo!"

Followed by, "No choice."

The swinging doors swallowed him. I stood alone in the endless hallway, powerless—choice-less and alone.

We attended church regularly almost as if by doing so I could control everything in our lives. I prayed but never so desperately as now. My prayers were sincere, but I expected more of myself than of my Lord.

"God, please. I need you now," I pleaded.

Robert, Damon's father, arrived. He said very little. Our conversations seldom came easily and often involved conflict, but now we were united in the profound desire for the wellbeing of our son. Silence spoke loudly in the tiny waiting room. An hour passed.

"He is lucky to be alive," the surgeon was speaking as he came through the door. "His ruptured appendix has splattered poison throughout his abdominal cavity and resulted in peritonitis, a severe infection. This could have been a deadly situation."

I never left Damon's hospital room. I slept curled-up on a two-seat uncomfortable sofa—when I slept. He wasn't going to have a snappy recovery. This time I couldn't kiss him and make him well. I couldn't make the pain go away. I laid my head next to his on the hospital bed, held his hand, and hid the expression on my face. He clung to me as I clung to the hope that he would respond to the medicines. The pain tortured his young body. Dark circles formed under his blue eyes. He wouldn't eat.

My aunt, Villa, came to visit and asked, "What would you like to eat if you could have anything in the world?"

A faint smile crossed Damon's glum face, "Pancakes," he replied.

She nodded and left. In short order she returned with a plate of homemade pancakes. Damon finally ate and licked the syrup from his lips.

Visitors came with gifts and get-well cards, many filled with cash. The room was soon adorned with helium-filled balloons and computer-generated signs.

"He must walk," the nurses insisted. The movement would jump start his system, but how could I cause him to suffer more? His young face twisted with the acute agony that every step caused.

Long and weary days passed before he could move without excruciating pain. He slowly seemed to improve. Five days later, he was released, and we went home—too soon. Two hours later, he was doubled over in severe pain with a urinary blockage.

"Bring him back. We will take care of your son," Dr. Forsyth told me on the phone. He seemed so sure. I had doubts. I was faltering as control slipped out of my hands again.

They readmitted him to the same room minus the decorations. Damon lay medicated, fragile, and still as a sleeping kitten. Specialists insisted that more tests were necessary.

I held back the tears that pooled in my eyes. They wheeled him off into another of the secret corridors of the hospital for an ultrasound. Globs of puss, like hail stones, were stuck throughout his lower abdominal cavity. Soon tubes and needles carried powerful antibiotics into his bruised arms.

I watched the drip, drip, drip of the IV willing the mysterious liquid to clean the poison from my boy's body. What next? Will he heal? Is there permanent damage? I was emotionally spent, no longer the mom in control. Fear had taken hold, and fatigue was its partner.

My dear friend, Tappy, came, "Come with me." She led me to the tiny chapel in the hospital and led me to the front pew, slid her arm around my shoulder, and prayed. The trust that I was in control, was gone. She prayed for Damon's recovery, and then she began to pray for my strength to return.

A force of words welled up and spilled from my mouth. I said aloud, "I am like the tree that grows by the living water. I may bend, but I will not break. I am like the tree," I repeated. I wasn't thinking about what I was saying. Words came without any effort on my part as if from a source beyond me. "Lord, you've carried me through before. I trust you are with me now." A peace wrapped itself around me and my hope started to return. My fears were replaced with peace, knowing the Lord was in control.

Tappy went home, and I went back to my son's room to remain for a few more days. When I slept, I kept one hand resting on Damon. He knew I was there for him and would not leave. Soon Damon was healing and pushing his IV cart up and down the halls. His bare bottom blinking from behind his hospital gown put a smile on the face of each nurse he passed. At last, he was well enough to leave the hospital for good.

Mother came to drive us home. As I packed our things, Damon whispered in Mom's ear. Then he grinned at me and said, "We'll be right back." He pulled her by the hand out the door towards the tiny gift shop that usually carried only candy, stuffed toys, and cards.

When Damon came back, he was grinning ear to ear. He used most of the cash he received to buy me a present. Neither he nor my mother knew the significance of this unlikely gift. I had not expected a love gift, especially this. He held out a box for me. More than a gift, it was a tangible token of a prayer received by heaven, a message that the Lord had heard my words in the chapel. I opened the box to find a shimmering, golden tree—a verification of God's presence.

According to Caroline Myss in *Entering the Castle*, her book based on writings of Sister Teresa of Avila,

"Everyone carries expectations of God. You expect God to answer your prayers. You expect a miracle if you pray long enough. You expect God to be fair, to be just, and to follow the rules of earthly law and order. You expect to see meaning and purpose in everything you do."

She goes on to say, "Expectations are the ego's way of holding God accountable. They block surrender and trust. What do you expect from God? Do you feel entitled to a job? To a home? To good health?"[43]

Prayer is not telling God what to do, but in prayer we often plead or bargain with God. Prayer is more than pleading; it's aligning our will with the Lord's. We must stop trying to understand God and stop trying to communicate with the Divine using our human understanding, seeking a cause and effect in all events.

I often hear well-meaning devout Christians say, "God has a reason," or "Everything happens for a reason." For us reason is all-important. That is a human's way of thinking, and yet we know, "My thoughts are not your thoughts. Neither are your ways my ways" (Isaiah 55:8, NIV). Myss states of Sister Teresa, "Teresa continually urges her readers to let go of the rational mind, to 'leave our reason and our fears' and surrender to divine love."[44] That is when faith is born.

In essence, prayer is surrendering. Why it is so difficult for us to let go of having things our way? Over my years as a Christian, I have prayed in various situations and in many different ways. Sometimes I pleaded. Other times I sent up a quick urgent request, but now I mostly abide. I find peace when I simply abide.

I find this acronym helpful for focusing in on the power of prayer:

P—Personal

E—Effortless

A—Acceptance of

C—Circumstances

E—Every day

Personal, effortless acceptance of circumstances each and every day. This doesn't mean that I don't call out to God. I am, after all, a mother. I exercise a way of praying as sharing with the Lord my deepest human desires while I continue to try to align my will with God's.

My prayers are often simple. Here are a few:

For dealing with a difficult person.

God,

Please give _____ an open heart, listening ears, and fill her/him with your love. Thank you for _____. Amen.

For my grown children:

Dear Father,

Please intervene in the lives of my all-grown-up children today.

Let the Holy Spirit intervene in their hearts in such a way that it is undeniable. Let all deceit be uncovered. Let every form of evil be recognized as such and protect them from it. Let love prevail and overcome all past hurts. Let understanding, grace, and forgiveness override all else. I trust you, Lord, with my children, the people I love most in this world. Amen.

From The Book of Common Prayer:

Almighty God, we entrust all who are dear to us to thy never-failing care and love, for this life and the life to come; knowing that thou art doing for them better things than we can desire or pray for; through Jesus Christ our Lord.

Amen.[45]

I find comfort from the words in this passage from *The Daily Word*, April 27, 2010:

If I am in need, I let my awareness of God's presence wash over me, calming me. I whisper reminders to myself: God is closer than my breath. Spirit is my comfort and my guidance. My fears and concerns melt away. My mind clears, and my heart steadies. God is my wellspring of support at all times. I move ahead now with confidence, for I know I am never alone. I live each day knowing that God guides me through both challenges and opportunities. Amen.[46]

This is my comfort in my distress, that your promise gives me life.
—Psalms 119:50 (New Revised Standard Version)

In spite of previously answered prayers, or evidence of God's work in our lives, we doubt. We doubt and we fear. We know the grass will grow green, the buds will appear, and the robins will come back in the spring, but still we doubt.

Jesus' message is clear, "Anyone who intends to come with me has to let me lead. You're not in the driver's seat; I am. Don't run from suffering; embrace it. Follow me and I'll show you how. Self-help is no help at all. Self-sacrifice is the way, my way, to saving yourself, your true self. What good would it do to get everything you want and lose you, the real you" (Matt 16:24-26, MSG).

Prayer is a two-way conversation. Knowing God's will in our life's situations requires listening as well as talking. We should come to God with an open heart, open ears, and open mind. If we treat prayer as we do a date with a friend or lover, we would come fully attentive, eager to be with our Lord and willing to follow God's lead.

I love what Philip Yancey says about prayer in his book, *Prayer: Does It Make Any Difference.* "In truth, what I think and feel as I pray, rather than the words I speak, may be the real prayer, for God 'hears' that too. My every thought occurs in God's presence. 'Before a word is on my tongue you know it completely, O Lord . . . Where can I flee from your presence? If I go up to the heavens, you are there; if I make my bed in the depths, you are there."[47]

As I learn to give voice to those secrets, mysteriously the power they hold over me melts away (Psalm 139:4, 7a–8, NIV).

As we embrace our path, we must also embrace the power of prayer as a support tool and lifeline. God loves us as a parent, so our Lord is not deaf to our plight, nor blind to our struggles. God is there every step of the way. We just need to call on our Lord for help, strength, and comfort.

SMORE TO CONSIDER

What are your feelings about prayer?

Don't need it   Not sure   I pray daily
   1 --- 2 --- 3 --- 4 --- 5 --- 6 --(7)-- 8 --- 9 --- 10

When you pray, what do you usually pray about?

[ ] Need help
[ ] Guidance or safety
[ ] Pour my heart out
[✓] Praise and gratitude
[ ] Other

Do you have a regular time of prayer in your life?

[✓] Yes[ ] No

Why, or why not?   NEED TO BE MORE
                        CONSISTENT

What are some of the things that get in the way of praying on a regular basis?   BUSINESS, OVERWHELMED
FATIGUE

Write about a time when you knew, without a doubt, that God answered your prayer(s). Remember to add the date, time, and place if you can.

CHAPTER TWELVE

Loving with Wisdom Gathered from Others

Life is a succession of lessons that must be lived to be understood.
—Helen Keller, *The Story of My Life*

Life requires that we learn—or suffer consequences. We start with simple lessons such as not touching the hot stove and progress to more complex lessons like the Golden Rule: "Do unto others as you would have them do to you." In other words, treat people with respect.

When we have troubles, sometimes, but not always, but sometimes, a spiritual lesson is underway. Many times, if you don't learn the first go-round, you will probably have another chance. Some lessons come to us more subtly than others. If we aren't paying attention and listening to that still small voice, we might miss a chance to learn a life lesson. I've experienced many second chances to learn lessons. The most difficult life experiences brought opportunities to learn. I found that I learned the most when teaching others.

It was not in my plan to become a teacher of the visually impaired. As a child, I directed plays in the backyard. Neighborhood kids were my cast. From a young age, I loved theater, so it was no wonder that I eventually became a drama teacher. Three children and a divorce later, I was teaching art and English, not my first choices. I thought if I could move to another city my life would have more promise. I could change career paths, get out of the classroom, and away from the stress of grading papers and disciplining teenagers. In the summer of 1989, I'd sent out my resume, made calls, and attempted to knock on as many doors as I could in order to find another position. Nothing, not even an interview, came of it.

When the time came to return to work for another school year, I was discouraged. Each night I knelt by my bed, weakened in spirit, weary to the bone, and said, "Lord, I must be where you want me. Please help me get through another day." Then I crawled into bed, collapsed, and hoped for a better tomorrow.

At this time, my children were fifteen, thirteen, and twelve, and the two boys were antsy and driving me nuts. I continued my nightly prayer ritual, growing increasingly frustrated, depressed, and almost angry.

October 6, 1989, marked a major turning point in my job situation. I found a tiny square note in my box at school. "See me after school. Byrd." It was from the superintendent.

Now what? I thought. Could I be in trouble? What for? It wasn't until I was in the superintendent's office, and his face broke into a familiar grin that I relaxed. He asked if I had a special education certification. He had to know I did not. He told me of a position that they needed to fill—teaching children who were blind, both in our school district and in a co-op with a neighboring district. It would require returning to college for additional certifications. He realized that was asking a lot.

Arrangements were made for me to spend a day with the teacher who was resigning. On Halloween Day, 1989, I went to several schools and was introduced to an entirely different world in education. I was intrigued by the prospects of such a major career change. The challenge of learning Braille forced me to think seriously about such an adjustment.

I had gone back to college once before with three children in tow, and I knew this would be even more difficult now that they were almost all teenagers. I had custody of all three children up until now. The boys had said for some time that they wanted to live with their dad full-time. There were no influential male figures in their lives. There was my mom, their older sister, and me, which didn't seem like the best arrangement for raising boys, but I couldn't bring myself to let them go.

During this period, I finally decided the boys might do better living with their dad. This wasn't an easy decision, and I experienced many emotions and difficulties over it for the next few years.

I was correct when I told the Lord that "I must be in the right place," having no idea this new career option was coming my way. I went back to college, got my certificate, and a new teaching position. It's true, we learn more by teaching, and over the years, I was going to learn so much from my new students.

On that introductory visit in October 1989, I met three-year-old Amanda. She was exceptionally articulate, and with great expression, she recited a Halloween poem for me. Her golden curls rested lightly on her tiny shoulders, (shoulders that would carry many burdens in the years ahead). Her adorable attitude, at least in part, was what drew me to accept the position of teaching the visually impaired for two school systems, which included numerous students on various campuses.

Amanda was born totally blind, a result of an inherited disorder. She was a bright student and attended regular classrooms, even though modifications had to be made in her lessons and materials. She was delightful most of the time, but other times she became frustrated with a world she couldn't see and didn't understand.

Her lack of understanding for the sighted and visual world caused her and the adults in her life problems. She didn't have much patience with sighted people. For instance, when told she must wear the clothes her mother set out for her to wear because they "matched," she would grumble as she stomped upstairs to change, "Sighted people and all this matching stuff!"

It wasn't easy for the elementary teachers who had Amanda in their classes, because Amanda lost her temper with teachers and classmates. She wanted help immediately when she needed it, unaware of any other students' needs or the circumstances around her. Often, I was called in to manage a difficult situation. Because of this, she and I developed a lasting bond.

After colliding with a child in the gym, Amanda pleaded, "I just want to run free, like everyone else." I explained that sighted people couldn't always see her coming because we cannot see behind us. She replied, "That's why I wish all of you had two sets of eyes." I was intrigued that she didn't see the issue as her inability to see at all but that of others inability to see more. Amanda and I had daily sessions where she could vent, and I just listened. This relieved her pent-up emotions. She dealt with so many difficulties.

One day I attempted to convey to Amanda the vast distance between the sun, the stars, and us. After a little thought she replied, "The earth is really as small as a piece of sand, and we just don't know it." Her sight was lacking, but her insights were profound.

On another occasion when Amanda was in second grade, it started to snow. Since this is so unusual where we live, all the children were allowed to go out to see if they could catch a snowflake. The discussion in the classroom that followed was about snowflakes and how beautiful and unique they are.

When Amanda came to me for instruction that day, she was somber. She said, "I wish I could see, just once, so I would know what they are talking about." I realized this independent little girl, was just that, a little girl with wishes and dreams just like other little girls. Some days she just needed a hug, and I gave her one.

I had the privilege of teaching Amanda to read, which of course, was Braille. One of her readers included the story of Stevie Wonder. As we read the story, it told of his troubled childhood, how poor his family was and how prejudice affected his life. Afterwards Amanda asked, "What is prejudice?"

Hoping to keep it simple I told her, "Some people have light-colored skin, and some have very dark-colored skin. Often the people with light skin are not nice to the people with dark skin."

She asked, "Why?"

"The light-colored people think they are better." I was wondering what meaning this would have for her. She thought for a bit then asked, "What color is my skin?" Answering her questions kept me alert.

The end of Amanda's first-grade year she asked, "Do you think God made a mistake when He made me born blind?"

"I don't think God makes mistakes," I replied. "He knew you would be special just the way you are."

"I am special, and I feel special," Amanda said confidently.

Over the years of answering Amanda's questions, she opened my eyes to "see" life differently. Her world had no skin color, only people, no outer beauty, only relationships. She had to touch her world to be part of it, I, too, realized that I had to touch my world to be part of it, maybe not in the same way as Amanda did, but I had to touch the hearts of the people in my life if I was to experience life to the fullest.

In spite of Amanda's difficulties over the years, she eventually became a tutor for calculus and physics, and even worked with a professor to write software for teaching other blind college students. In 2016, Amanda graduated with a BA in Computer Science from the University of Texas, Austin, with honors. As she says, "I struggle with many things." However, when she was given an IQ test, it was suggested she join Mensa. (Mensa, the high IQ society, provides a forum for intellectual exchange among its members.) She thought they had made a mistake. They had not. Today most of her friends are Mensa members. She is working on a PhD at A & M University.

When I became Kimberly's teacher, she was in the third grade. Kimberly was born with a birth defect called microphthalmia. She had tiny eyes that caused her to have extremely limited eyesight. Numerous surgeries were mostly unsuccessful. She wore a prosthesis (glass eye) in place of one of her eyes. The year after I began working with her, she had another retinal detachment resulting in her sixth surgery. All her remaining eyesight was lost. She was fitted for her second glass eye.

My job was to see that she received all the necessary modifications in the classroom, especially Braille materials. Kimberly was excellent with Braille, but Braille math, called the "Nemeth code" is complicated. If you have noticed the Braille in elevators, that is simple compared to the dots used in math. Up until then we managed her math lessons with enlarged sheets and magnification, but now we had to use Braille.

When Kimberly returned to school after her last surgery, I noticed she wasn't as sure of herself when it came to her new math lessons. I didn't want her to become discouraged after all she had been through, so I began to say things like, "Don't worry too much about catching on the first time through." and "There is plenty of time," and "No rush." Maybe I was too obvious. She picked up on my concern right away and replied, "Don't worry. I can learn this. I'm young." She approached most of life with this same optimism. She amazes me.

Another former student of mine, Leah, had some useful vision during her formative schooling, but during her college days she lost what little vision she had. It would be perfectly normal to feel like your life had just been derailed, but when she called me on the phone and told me of losing her remaining eyesight, I couldn't help but feel sad for her, but she was quick to say, "It's not so bad. I have a guide dog." She earned a BS degree in Emergency Management with a minor in public safety telecommunications (911 dispatching). She already holds several FEMA and Red Cross certificates. In January 2013, Leah married Aaron, and they had a baby boy, Josh. After a time, Leah and Aaron divorced, and Leah manages very well on her own. Leah is so inspiring.

On days when life has taken a bite out of my enthusiasm, I think of how my students handled the setbacks life had dealt them. I brush myself off and say, "It's not so bad." The power of optimism can take what could be a debilitating situation and turn it into an opportunity to become a superhero.

In the school where I worked, we had aides who stayed with the students. They were highly compassionate women who loved children and were eager to be helpful. It was sometimes difficult for the aides not to do too much for the students. It was a constant concern that the students not lose independence because an aide was assisting too much. The aides walked a tightrope as to when they should let the student struggle, or when they should lend a hand.

If you do too much for children, they develop something called, "learned helplessness." They actually believe they aren't capable of doing for themselves, and so they stop trying, paralyzing the natural growth of self-esteem. This can happen to all of us under the right circumstances.

When Kimberly was in middle school, we would have our daily meeting in a small room where we housed the brailling equipment. On one such day she dramatically pleaded with me to talk to her parents saying, "My parents are going to ruin my life!" Then she told me about her parents' plan to send her to a summer camp in Ruston, Louisiana, where they have facilities for children who are blind.

Apparently, one of the things they do at this summer camp to encourage independent mobility is to drop the student off on the opposite side of town and tell them to walk back. When I learned this, it terrified me, and I understood her panic. Granted, the people in Ruston are accustomed to seeing blind students with white canes, but to imagine our little Kimberly walking across town all alone, well, that seemed like too much to ask of a child to me.

Kimberly's parents did send her to camp, and she did have to walk back across town—as it turned out, it wasn't too much for Kimberly to handle. Even though it was stressful, Kimberly managed just fine. It was a life lesson that prepared her to later navigate the campus of Texas A&M University successfully—alone. This experience built her self-confidence and opened her mind to reach beyond her limitations. Kimberly went on to earn a degree in political science and psychology from Texas A&M University. She completed a policy internship for Senator Kay Bailey Hutchison, the former United States Senator from Texas, in Washington, D.C., and served a year as an AmeriCorps VISTA for the March of Dimes before earning a master's degree. She also received a PhD in Healthcare Management and Policy.

I could identify with Kimberly's fear of having to do something you don't think you can do because when I became a single mom, I felt like someone had dropped me off on the other side of town and told me to walk back blindfolded. I had no idea if I could do it or not, but with each step, I learned I was capable of things I never dreamed I could do. Sometimes the hardest situations in life build our self-esteem and a sense of independence that can't be developed any other way.

Laughter is good for us. As Proverbs 17:22 (New Living Translation) reminds us, "A cheerful heart is good medicine." It is a stress reliever, stimulates organs, and can improve your immune system. If nothing in your life seems funny make it a point to watch funny movies. Pull your children or girlfriends into the fun. There is nothing better than hearing children laugh or laughing with friends.

When Kimberly was in high school, we often met in the mornings in the Braille room. One morning I noticed she looked especially attractive. She was wearing makeup, even mascara. (I didn't realize it was the day for school pictures.) Wanting to encourage her I said, "You look great today. Your eyes are bright." To which she quickly retorted, "Yes, I know, we scrubbed them this morning."

Kimberly kept her quick wit that often took the edge off of awkward situations. Learning to laugh, even at ourselves, is an important way to keep our emotional health intact.

Ah! It is a great thing to have a sense of humor. To go through life without it . . . is like being in a wagon without springs. It's jolted by every pebble on the road.[48]

—Henry Ward Beecher

Being able to laugh can take away the heaviness of life. I have a paperweight on my desk that says: "Angels fly because they take themselves lightly." Humor and the ability to laugh at yourself can be of real benefit when facing personal struggles.

Our greatest weaknesses provide us with opportunities for growth that we might never have had otherwise. In 2 Corinthians 12:9, scripture says, "God's power is made perfect in our weakness" (NIV).

The students I taught who were blind demonstrated a courage that inspired me, that still inspires me to this day. They had an attitude of acceptance and faith. We often think of courage as bravery on a battlefield, and certainly, that is one type of courage, but facing an unknown future as a single mother, or a woman whose husband is not around to help, takes courage that rivals battlefield bravery.

Yes, my students may have missed many things all around them, but they were acutely aware of the important things of life because they had to face their fears and limitations. As they went on to live adult lives, some to marry and others to live independently, I witnessed courage that many sighted people do not possess. For the most part, they had no other choice but to move forward. The same could be true of raising children alone. Your choices may be limited, but your option to move forward with a good attitude can carry you through the toughest times.

As the head of your household, your approach to difficulties rubs off on your children. I guarantee you that others will catch your contagious attitude. Even if we feel like we are in the gutter, we still have the choice to look at the stars.

Deuteronomy 31:6 says, "Be strong and courageous. Do not be afraid or terrified because of them [your situation], for the Lord your God goes with you; he will never leave you nor forsake you" (NIV).

SMORE TO CONSIDER

Name a time of hardship that taught you a spiritual lesson.

Accepting my world is unfair, things can only be right in eternity

What was the hardship?

Passive minimizing scars from childhood can only be free it

What was the lesson? *I let go and let god*

to help me overcome my. Holding on to the weight can only prolong the pin

What limitations have changed the focus of your life?

dsylexia, ND.....

Name one positive outcome from that limitation.

Life is a journey; does every pebble jolt you on your path? Have you developed learned helplessness?

[/] Yes[ ] No

What things should you start doing for yourself that you allow others to do for you? Name two:

1. *decisions / self belief*
2. *affirmalia.*

Name the last time you had a good laugh—what was it about?

Comedy general conversations

Do you feel strong and courageous?

[ ] Yes [/] No

Appendices

Appendix 1

Chaos, the Messenger A Spiritual Exercise in Alone Times

"Chaos is always a messenger. Sometimes its message is hugely significant; at other times it is a lesser but still valuable insight," according to Caroline Myss, the author of *Entering the Castle*, which is a modern-day take on Sister Teresa of Àvila's *The Interior Castle*.

You may think that there is absolutely nothing good that can come from the chaos you are living. I have no intention of minimizing the troubles you face. They are real. They may be very messy, troubling, disastrous, or just aggravating. Maybe you are facing a crisis that demands immediate attention. Perhaps yours is an ongoing saga that seems to have no end.

Here is a guide from an old bird that has built and abandoned many a nest and fought off more than her share of predators. Find a way to carve out a few minutes of time alone. You may have to plant the kids in front of the TV while you lock yourself in the bathroom. You will need: a match and candle, paper and pen, a highlighter, and a Bible.

- Light the candle. This is to keep you focused.

- Sit comfortably.

- Read Psalms 25:5 aloud as an opening prayer. I prefer to read from my own Bible, but here is the text for you if you need it handy:

"Guide me in your truth and teach me, for you are God my Savior, and my hope is in you all day long."

- On the paper, write headings for two columns: "Immediate Attention" and "Long-term Issues."

- Write the thoughts as they come to your mind. Don't think too long.

- When you have filled the page or completed your list, take a breath and read it aloud to yourself.

- Highlight the words that stand out to you.

- Does any theme appear? Are there any reoccurring words?

- Read Jeremiah 29:11-13 (NIV) aloud:

"For I know the plans I have for you," declares the Lord, "plans to prosper you and not to harm you, plans to give you hope and a future. Then you will call on me and come and pray to me, and I will listen to you. You will seek me and find me when you seek me with all your heart."

- Turn paper over and number lines 1-5.

- Next to number 1, write any message that seems to come through in "Immediate Attention" list.

- Next to number 2, write any second message that appeared.

- Next to number 3, write what you sense you are to do? What action should you take?

- Next to number 4, write what you sense you should do with the second message.

- Next to number 5, write how you will go about taking action.

- Read James 2:14-17 (NIV) aloud:

What good is it, my brothers and sisters, if someone claims to have faith but has no deeds? Can such faith save them? Suppose a brother or a sister is without clothes and daily food. If one of you says to them, "Go in peace; keep warm and well fed," but does nothing about their physical needs, what good is it? In the same way, faith by itself, if it is not accompanied by action, is dead. Think on this: Out of the darkest day on earth, the crucifixion, came the resurrection.

Close your session by reading John 14:25-27 (MSG) aloud:

I'm telling you these things while I'm still living with you. The Friend, the Holy Spirit whom the Father will send at my request, will make everything plain to you. The Holy Spirit will remind you of all the things I have told you. I'm leaving you well and whole. That's my parting gift to you. Peace. I don't leave you the way you're used to being left— feeling abandoned, bereft. So don't be upset. Don't be distraught.

When you have struggles, consider that they might be bringing a message. Embrace them. Trust the Spirit to lead you to the message meant just for you.

Appendix II

Going Deeper with the Enneagram

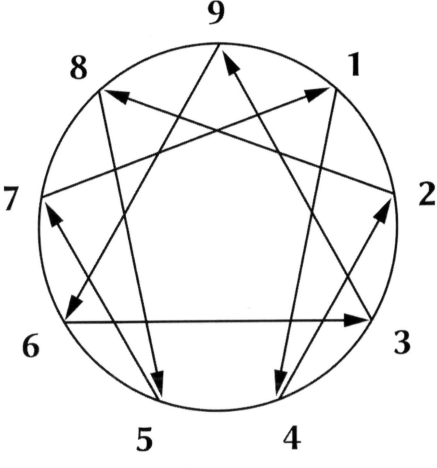

Enneagram

I have studied the Enneagram through books, CDs, and Suzanne Stabile's workshops, and I find it to be exceptional. It's especially valuable for those wanting to go deeper into a spiritual transformative self-study. For more information on the Enneagram, please visit: The Enneagram Institute https://www.enneagraminstitute.com

For Stabile's Enneagram workshops, please visit https://
suzannestabile.com/.Suzanne and her husband, Rev. Joe founded and run
the Life in the Trinity Ministry in Dallas, TX.

For more information on Suzanne ministry,
please visit: https://lifeinthetrinity.com

The Enneagram, at its core, helps us to see ourselves at a
deeper, more objective level and can be of invaluable assistance on our
path to self-knowledge.[49]

Appendix III

Boundaries Are For Your Protection

A page to print and put in front of you and read aloud daily.

"Boundaries define us. They define what is me and what is
not me. A boundary shows me where I end and someone else begins,
leading me to a sense of ownership. Knowing what I am to own and
take responsibility for gives me freedom. Taking responsibility for my
life opens up many different options. Boundaries help us keep the
good in and the bad out. Setting boundaries inevitably involves taking
responsibility for your choices. You are the one who makes them. You are
the one who must live with their consequences. And you are the one who
may be keeping yourself from making the choices you could be happy
with. We must own our own thoughts and clarify distorted thinking."[50]

—Henry Cloud
From *Boundaries* by Dr. Henry Cloud and Dr. John Townsend

Appendix IV

Experiencing Loss

Experiencing loss is one of the most common things we will go
through throughout every season of our lives. It is part of the defining
process of what makes a season memorable and impacting. It is the
opportunity to develop the skills of becoming an overcomer. Most loss

experiences are manageable and can be overcome with reasonable effort. However, there are losses that will require us to dig deeper inside of ourselves. When we find ourselves in a loss of significant depth, we may question our faith in God. In actuality, it is our faith in ourselves that is being challenged. Our faith in God and our faith in ourselves will have a greater refinement when we reach a place of maturity and completion.

There are a few definitions that may help us understand things better. Bereavement means to be set apart from. This separation can leave us with a void or emptiness. The void is filled with the emotions. Grief is the emotions that we feel during a season of loss. Mourning is the expression of those emotions of grief. Tears can be a common source of mournful expressions.

I often remind those who reach out for coaching during times of great loss that there are a few truths to keep in mind. To begin with, this is not our first loss. It is just our worst loss. Thus, we have been here before. Our lifetime of lower-level losses has been preparing us for this most painful season of our life. We are more prepared than we know. Another truth that I share is that we only grieve what we love. We do not grieve what we do not love. We see tragedy and loss all the time. Though we may empathize with others, the loss is not as impacting because of the lower measure of love. Therefore, we never stop grieving because we never stop loving those most precious to us. The heaviness of a difficult loss will subside, but we never want grief to leave completely because of its ingredient of love. As we process the emotions of grief, we take extra care to proceed with honorable expressions and behaviors for the loved one that meant so much to us.

Divorce has its own unique grief. Though this may not be a literal death. This is a great loss all the same. These may include the loss of the original family unit that gives us joy, the loss of the hope of fulfilling the dreams that we spent creating together, and the loss of the levels of security that the adult relationship once gave us. The same feelings of being overwhelmed with the unfamiliar experiences and with other vulnerabilities exist during divorce as they do in death. These feelings are often accompanied by the negative feelings for the previous spouse. This often requires those going through a divorce to dig deeper within themselves to suppress their natural instinct to react to these difficult feeling so that they may develop and apply more productive responses. Death may have the pain of permanence. Divorce may have a more lingering effect because of the slow unraveling of the tapestry of marriage and family.

The coping strategies to rebuild self-confidence, and to accomplish peace of mind, apply to both death and divorce. Grievers of either type of loss will have voids to fill and regrets to remedy. The challenges that we are called to accept are to remain in a constant state of adjustment to promote achievements. This includes achievements in our personal and professional lives. As well as learning to love ourselves and love others in ever better ways. As mentioned, loss brings the opportunity to always be better.

— Charles L. Olliff, M.Ed., LPC
Creator and Facilitator of the "Getting Better Grief Group"
https://www.chuckolliff.org/

Appendix V

Becoming Self-Aware on a Deeper Level

The following resources contain valuable information on how to become more self-aware.

Circle of Hope with Suzanne Stabile
https://www.circleofhope.net/blog/self-reflecting-and-awareness-the-enneagram-with-suzanne-stabile/

"At Work with the Enneagram"
https://youtu.be/kdoHSebJAP8

"Find Wholeness and Balance with the Enneagram:"
https://youtu.be/zI4YEW_xABQ

Appendix VI

Budgeting Matters
by Elsa Kok Colopy

Budgeting does matter for each of us, no matter what our income. But maybe you're like me, and you need some added incentive to go through the effort. If so, think on these things.

Pay off debt. Debt robs us. Not only does it rob us financially of the interest we pay, but it also robs us of our emotional well-being. On too many occasions, I've been irritable with my daughter, Sami, because the credit card bill was due. She didn't have a thing to do with it, but she paid the price (pun intended) with my attitude. Having a clean slate will definitely take a load off your emotional and financial shoulders. Budgeting will help bring that to pass.

Build an emergency savings. One thing budgeting taught me was that paying myself was as important as paying off creditors. As I set a monthly plan, I made savings a bill that I paid too. Granted, it was a very small bill, but I still paid it. And it came in handy—like the time I was singing in my car, hit the curb, and needed a new tire; or when my washing machine broke; or when my dog ate a foreign object and needed the vet. Budgeting will help you set up a fund to take care of those not-so-every-day expenses.

Know where your money goes. I was surprised to discover how much money I spent on stupid stuff. I thought I wasn't spending anything—but as I kept track, I found that I spent money on fast food, coffee from the convenience store, movie rentals, and the occasional junk food spree that turned out to be more than occasional. As I realized how much cash was going out for items I'd never see again, I determined to cut back. Fries didn't constitute a necessary food item (no matter how much Sami disagreed).

Set aside fun money. Once I had a budget set up, I could put away a little money weekly for fun stuff. Instead of the quick output for fast food or a movie rental, I could save for a few weeks and actually take Sami on a little overnight or to a dinner and a real movie theater (where our feet stuck to the buttery floor and everything).

Wahoo!

Watch your income grow. The wonderful thing about budgeting is that once you have a budget in place, you can keep it in place as your income grows. When you become that rich and famous rock star or best-selling novelist, you'll have the skills to handle your newfound wealth. Budgeting is a great tool to have—and as your income grows with time, you'll have a good handle on your finances. elsacolopy@gmail.com

Resources: https://www.ramseysolutions.com/budgeting/budgeting-tips-for-single-moms

Appendix VII

Thoughts on Waiting

The following articles contain helpful information for your journey as a single mom.

- Waiting as a Single Mom: https://letslivebright.com/2021/06/09/waiting-as-a-single-mom/
- Waiting on God When It's No Fun: https://justmoved.org/waiting-on-god/

Appendix VIII

Teaching Morals Builds Your Childs Character Resources:

- 15 Ways to Raise a Child with Great Values: https://www.ahaparenting.com/read/values
- 10 Values You Should Teach Your Young Child: https://empoweredparents.co/values-to-teach-your-child/

Manners and Empathy:

- 8 Ways to Instill Manners in Your Child Without Even Trying: https://www.parents.com/parenting/better-parenting/ways-to-instill-manners-in-your-child-without-even-trying/

- 6 Ways to Teach Kids to Be Kind: https://www.parents.com/kids/development/social/teaching-kids-to-be-kind/

"Ages and Stages: Empathy"

- Ages and Stages of Empathy: https://nycpreschool.org/helpful-preschool-resources/parents/resources/pharetra-nullam-justo-risus-egestas/

- 22 Simple Manners All Kids Should Know: https://www.parents.com/kids/development/social/25-manners-kids-should-know/

Appendix IX

Fun with Your Kids Creates Great Memories

50 Fun Activities for Single Moms https://thelifeofasinglemom.com/50-fun-activities-for-single-moms-by-kris-swiatocho by Kris Swiatocho

Kris is a highly regarded leader in ministries to Christian singles. You may reach her at https://krisswiatochoministries.org.

She is also the co-author of Intentional Relationships for Singles, which is a 12-week Bible study.

Summertime Activities for Single Moms and Kids by Pam Kanaly. Pam is the co-founder of the Arise Ministry in Oklahoma. Learn more about her at https://www.arisesinglemoms.com/speakers/pam-kanaly/

Resources: https://thefamilydinnerproject.org

Appendix X

Stages of Faith Show Spiritual Growth
By Brian McLaren[51]

	SIMPLICITY	COMPLEXITY	PERPLEXITY	HARMONY
ATTITUDE TOWARDS PRESENT STAGE	This is the only correct or orthodox stage	This is the most effective and exciting stage	This stage is tough, sometimes miserable, but more honest than the previous stages	This stage will become a new simplicity, followed by a new complexity, etc.; the growth process never ends
ATTITUDE TOWARDS TRADITION	Faith in an authoritative tradition	Faith in a useful or helpful tradition	Doubt in a corrupt or damagin tradition	Faith and doubt in an evolving tradition
ATTTIDUE TOWARDS DOUBT	Doubt is a failure, weakness, defection, betrayal or sin	Doubt is a problem to be solved or sickness to be cured	Doubt is a virtue to be cultivated	Doubt is a necessary part of life, a portal from one stage to another
FAITH AND DOUBT	Faith before doubt	Faith managing doubt	Faith in doubt	Faith and doubt in creative tenstion
FAITH IS...	Assent to required beliefs	Means to desired ends	An obstacle to critical thinking	A humble, reverent openness to mystery that expresses itself in non-discriminatory love

Appendix XI

Prayer is Your Source of Strength

What Phillip Yancey says about his book, *Prayer: Does It Make Any Difference?* Prayer can be frustrating, confusing, and fraught with mystery. I probe such questions as:

- Is God listening? Why should God care about me?
- If God knows everything, what's the point of prayer?
- How can I make prayer more satisfying?
- Why do so many prayers go unanswered?
- Do prayers for healing really matter?
- Does prayer change God?

I began with a list of such questions, then I studied all 650 prayers in the Bible and interviewed scores of people about their own experiences with prayer. The process of writing caused a revolution in my own conception and practice of prayer. I now see it not so much as a way of getting God to do my will as a way of being available to get in the stream of what God wants to accomplish on earth.[52]

Appendix XII

The Best Lessons are Learned from a Child
by Kay Miller

It was a summer Sunday morning, which meant I was rolling two sleepyheads out of bed for church. We were up early, getting dressed for Sunday school. I was trying to ignore the warning signs of a migraine headache approaching. We brushed teeth, combed hair, got dressed, and drove to church. By the end of the service, my migraine was in full swing. I knew I wouldn't even be attempting to cook lunch—I needed a dark, cool room and some peace and quiet, and I needed it NOW!

I pulled thru a Burger King, ordered both boys cheeseburgers, fries, and drinks and headed back home. We changed out of our church clothes. I unwrapped their burgers, settled them down at the kitchen table and then went to get the ketchup from the refrigerator. When I returned to the table, my oldest son was picking the seeds off the top of his bun. I asked what he was doing, and he replied, "Well, these are hamburger seeds, so I'm gonna plant them in the backyard and grow me a hamburger tree!" I knew in that moment I had birthed a son with an entrepreneurial mindset!

I couldn't help but compare sesame seeds to mustard seeds in that moment. Mason possessed the ability to see the smallest seeds and imagine the greatest return on them. According to the good book, we are all given a measure of faith (Matthew 17:20). We are told if we have faith the size of a mustard seed, we can move a mountain! That verse goes on to say nothing is impossible if we have faith.

As a single mom, having faith is a struggle at times. The day-to-day juggling of being both mom and dad, along with financial strains, conflicting schedules with extracurricular activities, and school—you just run out of steam. Your faith is tested, along with your sanity, your peace, your joy—it's all consumed by the reality of not being able to be all things to your children. If we could truly grasp the impact we make on our children, and then recognize the impact they make on us. In that moment, standing at the kitchen table, overtaken by the pain of a headache, I believe God spoke to me through my seven-year-old son. He challenged me to believe great things from small faith.

Be encouraged today—keep your faith, even if it's so small you can barely see it. Plant that seed of faith, water it with your prayers and tears—and it will grow! You will grow, too, and your children will one day understand and believe for themselves because their mom (and/or dad) never lost sight of their faith, in all situations and circumstances.

Pianogirl.miller@gmail.com

Endnotes

1   Single Mother Statistics
https://singlemotherguide.com/single-mother-statistics/
https://www.census.gov/data/tables/2021/demo/families/cps-2021.
html

2   Silverstein, Shel. The Missing Piece Meets the Big O. New York, NY 1981. Print

3   Wilkinson, Bruce. The Dream Giver. Sisters, Oregon: Multnomah, 2003.

4   Marano, Hara Estroff. "What is Solitude?" Psychology Today. July 1, 2003. Web. 16 April 2015.

5   Chambers, Oswald. My Utmost for His Highest: Selections for the Year: The Golden Book of Oswald Chambers. Westwood, NJ: Barbour, 1993. Print.

6   Brown, C. Brené. The Gifts of Imperfection: Let Go of Who You Think You're Supposed to Be and Embrace Who You Are. Center City, MN: Hazelden, 2010. Print. 39.

7   Cloud, Henry, and John Sims Townsend. Boundaries: When to Say Yes, When to Say No to Take Control of Your Life. Grand Rapids, MI: Zondervan Pub. House, 1992. Print. 224.

8   "Orison Swett Marden Quotes." BrainyQuote. n.d. Web. 16 April 2015.

9   Carter, Jay. Nasty People: How to Stop Being Hurt by Them without Becoming One of Them. Chicago: Contemporary, 1989. Print. 16.

10   Robbins, Kathryn and Cooper, Cassandra (2014). What Makes You Tick. Archer's Press, St. Louis, MO. Print.

11   Buscaglia, Leo F., and Steven Short. Living, Loving and Learning. Thorofare, NJ: C.B. Slack, 1982. Print

12   https://quoteinvestigator.com/2018/04/01/life-goes/

13   Bertshausen, Roger. Beyond Absence: A Treasury of Poems, Quotations, and Readings on Death and Remembrance. Boston: Skinner

House, 2006. Print.

14   https://thisemotionallife.org/blogs/7-steps-overcome-your-divorce/
     7 Steps to Overcome Your Divorce. Debra Warner This Emotional
     Life. PBS Online. Web. 16 April 2015.

15   https://thisemotionallife.org/blogs/7-steps-overcome-your-divorce/
     Ibid Fredda Wassermann

16   "Eleanor Roosevelt Quotes." Brainy Quote. n.d. Web. 16 April 2015.

17   "Ella Wheeler Wilcox." GoodReads. n.d. Web. 16 April 2015.

18   "Miguel de Cervantes Saavedra." GoodReads. n.d. 16 April 2015.

19   Littauer, Florence. Your Personality Tree: Discover the Real You by
     Uncovering the Roots Of . . . Waco, TX: Word, 1986. Print. 94.

20   Davis, Janet. The Feminine Soul: Surprising Ways the Bible Speaks to
     Women. Colorado Springs, CO: NavPress, 2006. Print. 214.

21   Stoltz, Paul Gordon, and Erik Weihenmayer. The Adversity Advan-
     tage: Turning Everyday Struggles into Everyday Greatness. New York:
     Fireside/Simon & Schuster, 2006. Print. 15.

22   Ibid, Stoltz, Paul Gordon, and Erik Weihenmayer, 55.

23   Buckingham, Marcus, and Donald O. Clifton. Now, Discover Your
     Strengths. New York: Free, 2001. Print. 3.

24   "Saint Francis de Sales Quotes." BrainyQuote. n.d. 16 April 2015.

25   Thoreau, Henry David. "Thoreau Reader." Thoreau Eserver, n.d. Web.
     17 April 2015.

26   Behrendt, Greg, and Liz Tuccillo. He's Just Not That Into You: Gal-
     lery Books, 2009.

27   Chambers, Oswald. My Utmost for His Highest: Selections for the
     Year: Westwood, NJ: Barbour, 1993. Print.

28   Howe, Michele, and Christopher A. Foetisch. Burdens Do a Body
     Good: Meeting Life's Challenges with Strength (and Soul). Peabody,
     MA: Hendrickson, 2010. Print.

29   Miley, Jeanie. Joint Venture: Practical Spirituality for Everyday Pil-
     grims. Macon, GA: Smyth & Helwys Pub., 2011. Print. 70.

30   "Margaret Walker Quotes." BrainyQuote, n.d. Web. 17 April 2015.

31   "Henry James." BrainyQuote.com. Xplore Inc, 2015. 30 April 2015.

32   Kapp, Diane. "Raising Children with an Attitude of Gratitude." The
     Wall Street Journal. N.p., 3 Dec. 2013. Web. 17 Apr. 2015.

33   https://www.brainyquote.com/Xplore 2015. April 30 2015
     http://www.brainyquote.com/quotes/quotes/g/georgebern107004.
     html George Bernard Shaw.

34   The Road Not Taken Robert Frost Poetry Foundation. Poetry Foun-

dation, n.d. Web. 30 Apr. 2015.

35 http://www.brainyquote.com/quotes/quotes/c/carljung125713.html
    BrainyQuote.com. Xplore Inc, 2015. 30 April 2015.

36 Pope, Alexander. "An Essay on Man." The Norton Anthology of English Literature: The Restoration and the Eighteenth Century. 8th ed. Vol. 1. New York, NY: W.W. Norton, n.d. 2007.

37 Marshall, Catherine. Adventures in Prayer. Chappaqua, NY: Chosen, 1975. Print.

38 McWilliams, Peter (n.d.). Retrieved from http://www.quotationspage.com/quotes.

39 Al-Anon Family Group. One Day at a Time in Al-Anon (1973). Don Mills, Canada: T.

40 http://chrisfieldblog.com/ Blind Helen Howarth Lemmel Turns Our Eyes. N.p., 14 Nov. 2008. Web. 30 Apr. 2015.

41 Morgan, Robert J. "Turn Your Eyes Upon Jesus." Then Sings My Soul. Nashville, TN: Thomas Nelson, 2004. 282. Print.

42 Fosdick, Harry Emerson. The Meaning of Prayer. New York, Association Press, 1916.

43 https://www.myss.com/entering-the-castle/overview/

44 Ibid. Myss, Caroline M., 212.

45 The Book of Common Prayer (1928). Justus Anglican. Retrieved from Justus.anglican.org/resources/ (17 April 2015).

46 The Daily Word (2010, April 27) Retrieved from http://www.daily-word.com

47 Yancey, Philip. Prayer: Does It Make Any Difference? Grand Rapids, MI: Zondervan, 2006. 103.

48 http://www.brainyquote.com/quotes/quotes/h/henrywardb161732.html Henry Ward Beecher

49 https://www.enneagraminstitute.com/about

50 Cloud, Henry, and John Sims Townsend. Boundaries: When to Say Yes, When to Say No to Take Control of Your Life. Grand Rapids, MI: Zondervan Pub. House, 1992. Print. 224.

51 Stages of Faith Show Spiritual Growth By Brian McLaren

52 Yancey, Philip Prayer: Does It Make Any Difference? Grand Rapids, MI: Zondervan, 2006. 103. Print.

Acknowledgements

A huge thanks goes to Kathryn Robbins who was like a midwife for me when the book was first birthed. April Cox made it possible for me to go through the process, step-by-step, and showed me what I didn't know how to do.

A shout out of appreciation to all the single mothers I've taught and coached who were open and willing to grow spiritually.

A hug goes to my former students who were willing to share with me.

About the Author

Gail Cawley Showalter loves to encourage women who are hurting, particularly single moms. She is the founder of SMORE for Women: Single Mothers—Overjoyed, Rejuvenated, Empowered.

Gail is a moving, heartwarming, and genuine speaker and storyteller. Her passion is to encourage women to discover and develop their abilities and inner strengths.

Gail was a single mother of three for sixteen years before she married her husband Sam in 1996. She knows the struggles, the heartaches, and the day-to-day difficulties of being single and head of a household. During her years as a single mom, she learned to depend on the Lord for guidance. Though she is happily remarried, her heart's desire is to offer seeds of guidance to single moms.

Her inspiring articles have appeared in Focus on the Family's *Single Parent Family, Valley Living for the Whole Family,* and *LIVE, a Weekly Journal of Practical Christian Living.* She also has stories in the book, by Marita Littauer, and by Melissa Howell and Angela Peters.

Along with her coaching credentials, Gail holds a Master's degree from The University of Texas and worked in public education for twenty years. She makes her home in Nederland, Texas, with her husband Sam. They each have three grown children and, together, fourteen grandchildren.

Gail acts as an advisor for SMORE for Women and produces online courses.